다문화가족 학부모를 위한 가이드 북

The Guidebook for the Parents of Multi-cultural Families

(주) 교육과세상

✿ 들어가는 말

1990년대 이후 국제결혼의 양적 팽창이 이루어지면서 다문화가정이 급증하고 있습니다. 국제결혼으로 이루어진 다문화가정은 서로 다른 문화적 배경을 가지고 있기 때문에 한국생활의 초기 적응에 있어서 정신적, 신체적으로 많은 갈등이 나타나게 됩니다. 그중에서 가장 어려운 것이 언어 소통의 문제로 여성결혼이민자 자신만의 문제가 아니라 자녀 양육에서도 많은 어려움을 겪고 있는 것이 현실입니다.

대한민국에 사는 모든 어린이들은 만6세가 되면 누구나 초등교육을 받아야 할 의무가 있습니다. 자녀의 원만한 학교생활을 도와주며, 자녀의 잠재력과 가능성을 키워 주는 현명한 학부모가 되기 위해 많은 노력이 필요할 때에 다문화가정의 어머니들은 언어소통의 문제로 자녀들과의 대화부족 · 취학관련 정보부족으로 불안감이 가득합니다.

이러한 문제점을 조금이나마 덜어 주기 위해 초등학교 1학년 취학 자녀를 둔 다문화가정의 학부모를 위한 가이드북을 자국어로 번역 제공함으로써 학부형이 된다는 설렘에 대해 아이에 대한 기대와 교육에 대한 자신감을 가질 수 있는 기회가 되고자 합니다.

교재구성은
첫째마당에서는 취학 준비시기에 알아야 할 내용
둘째마당은 취학 전 길러줘야 할 생활습관
셋째마당은 취학 전 알아야 할 학습내용
넷째마당은 취학 후 알아야 할 내용
다섯째마당은 도움이 되는 정보로 구성하였습니다.

초등학교 1학년은 학부모님의 관심이 많이 필요로 하는 시기입니다. 아이 스스로 문제를 해결할 수 있도록 올바르고 일관된 방향으로 교육 하며, 다른 사람들과 더불어 사는 방법을 배울 수 있도록 함과 동시에 경험과 체험을 통해 학습에 대한 흥미를 유발할 수 있도록 자녀를 이끌어 줄 수 있는 현명하고 지혜로운 다문화 가정의 학부모가 되시는데 도움이 되기를 바랍니다.

Introduction

The number of multi-cultural families has been rapidly increasing due to the increase in the number of international marriages since the 1990's. Multi-cultural families are comprised of different cultural backgrounds so that a great deal of physical and psychological distress is most likely to be exhibited during the early stages of adjustment to Korean life. Of the many difficulties, the language barrier is the hardest, and it is not just a problem to the immigrant married women but also a difficult reality for couples to raise children.

It is mandatory for all children to receive primary education in Korea. It is a critical time for parents to be wise about putting their best efforts in helping their children to have a amicable school life, fostering their children's potential and possibilities. However, the parents of the multi-cultural families sense tremendous anxiety because of the Korean language barrier with their children and the lack of information about sending them to school.

To help take off some of the burden, this book will serve as a way of meeting parents' education expectations for their children, and gain confidence in education and experience the thrill of becoming a school parent by providing a school guidebook written in the languages of multi-cultural families who have children entering school.

Composition of the Textbook :

The first chapter has information on admission preparation.
The second chapter has information on the lifestyle that their child should have before entering school.
The third chapter has information on the learning content that their child should acquire before entering school.
The fourth chapter has information that the parents of the school-aged child should know about after the admission of their child.
The fifth chapter is comprised of helpful information.

In the first year of elementary school children require a great deal of attention from their parents. Children need to be educated in an appropriate and consistent manner so that they will be equipped with autonomous problem solving skills, in other words, to learn to live with others, and to get them interested in studying through hands-on experiences. We hope that this guidebook will help you become judicious and wise school parents of your multi-cultural family.

차례

첫째마당
취학 준비시기에 알아야 할 내용   06
1. 취학통지서
2. 취학 유예
3. 조기 입학
4. 신입생 예비소집
5. 입학식과 반 배정
6. 입학 전 건강 확인
7. 취학준비물

둘째마당
취학 전 길러줘야 할 생활습관   24
1. 일찍 일어나기
2. 바른 식습관 갖기
3. 등하굣길 익히기
4. 공손한 인사예절
5. 사교성 키우기
6. 물건 관리하기
7. 정리정돈 잘하기
8. 뛰지 않기
9. 화장실 사용법
10. 제대로 손 씻기
11. 책상에 앉아 있는 습관 기르기
12. 준비물 · 과제물 혼자서 챙기는 습관 기르기
13. 컴퓨터 사용 습관

셋째마당
취학 전 알아야 할 학습내용   38
1. 초등학교 학습, 달라진 점 세 가지
2. 선행학습 집착은 금물
3. 학교 수업준비
4. 영어 수학보다는 한글 독서 교육이 중요
5. 기초학습

넷째마당
취학 후 알아야 할 내용   48
1. 학교에서의 하루일과
2. 알림장
3. 가정환경 조사서 작성법
4. 결석, 지각, 조퇴
5. 전학
6. 재량 활동 시간
7. 특별 활동 시간
8. 특기 적성 교육 활동 시간
9. 현장 체험 학습
10. 급식
11. 그림일기 지도법
12. 학부모가 참여할 수 있는 단체
13. 학부모 오리엔테이션과 학부모회의
14. 스쿨뱅킹과 홈페이지 등록
15. 방학을 효율적으로 보내는 방법

다섯째마당
도움이 되는 정보   72
1. 입학 후 가장 많은 문제점과 해결법
2. 대답하기 곤란한 질문들
3. 전문가들이 들려주는 초등학교 1학년 학부모를 위한 지침
4. 우리아이 우등생 만들기 십계명
5. 내 아이, 준비된 리더로 키우기 위한 10가지 전략
6. 참고 사이트와 도서

Contents

Chapter 1
Things You Need to Know About the Admission to School   06

1. School admission notice
2. Admission postponement
3. Early admission
4. School tour day
5. Admission ceremony and assigning classes
6. Health check-up prior to the admission
7. School supplies for starting school

Chapter 2
The Types of Lifestyle Their Child Should Have Before Entering School   24

1. Getting up early
2. Becoming familiar with the routes from and to school
3. Acquainting the road to school
4. Polite etiquette
5. Fostering sociability
6. Keeping personal belongings
7. Pick-up and organizing
8. Not running around
9. Using a bathroom
10. Thoroughly washing hands
11. Fostering habits of sitting at a desk
12. Fostering habits of self-preparing school materials and doing home-work
13. Habits of using a computer

Chapter 3
Learning Content Your Child Should Acquire Before Entering School   38

1. Three changes in elementary school study
2. No Preview
3. Preparing school lessons
4. The importance of weighing heavier on Korean reading than English or math.
5. Basic study

Chapter 4
What Parents Should Know After the Admission of Their Child   48

1. Daily activities at school
2. Notice
3. Reporting method on family background
4. Absence, late, early leave
5. Transfer
6. Discretion activity time
7. Extracurricular activity time
8. The specialty and aptitude education activity time
9. Field trip
10. School meals
11. The methods of teaching the picture diary
12. Organizations the school parents can join
13. School parents' orientation and meeting
14. School banking and school web site registration.
15. Ways to have productive vacations

Chapter 5
Other Useful Information   72

1. The most frequent problems and the solutions after entering school
2. Questions difficult to answer
3. Specialists' advice to school parents of the first graders
4. Ten commandments to make my child an honor student.
5. 10 strategies to raise my child to become a prepared leader
6. Other reference sites and books

취학 준비시기에 알아야 할 내용

2009학년도부터는 취학 기준일이 1월 1일로 변경되어 1월 1일생부터 12월 31일생까지 한 학년에 입학하게 됩니다. 즉, 2010년에 입학이 가능한 아이는 2003년 1월 1일생부터 2003년 12월 31일생입니다. 2003년 1,2월 생 중 입학 유예를 했던 아이들과 2004년도에 태어났지만 조기 입학을 희망하는 아이도 함께 입학할 수 있습니다.

학부모들은 취학 적령기 전후 1년 범위 내에서 교장선생님의 심사 없이도 취학 선택권을 결정 할 수 있게 됨으로서 부모의 책임이 커져 신중하게 결정해야 합니다.

만약 조기입학이나 입학유예를 원한다면 학부모가 10월 1일부터 12월 31일까지 관할 주민자치센터에 신고하여야 취학 통지에 포함시켜 주거나 제외시켜 줍니다.

1. 취학통지서

1월 말에서 2월 초 사이에 취학 통지서를 나누어 줍니다

취학 통지서는 아이가 학교에 갈 나이(만 6세) 되었다는 것을 알리는 문서입니다. 취학 학교가 정해지면 각 읍·면·동사무소에서는 '취학 학교, 예비 소집일, 입학식 날짜' 등이 적힌 취학 통지서를 1월 말부터 2월 초에 취학 대상 아동이 있는 가정에 나누어 줍니다.

만약 이 기간에 취학 통지서를 받지 못했다면 읍·면·동사무소에 꼭 확인해야 하며 각 가정으로 배부된 취학 통지서는 잘 관리했다가 예비소집일에 학교에 제출해야 합니다.

또한, 취학 통지서를 받으면 2월 10일을 전후해 있는 신입생 예비소집과 3월 초에 있는 입학식 날짜를 꼭 기록해 둬서 빠지는 일이 없도록 해야 합니다.

Things You Need to Know About the Admission to School

The basic date for entering school has been changed to January 1st, so that children born between January 1st and December 31st enter school in the same grade. In other words, the children who start school in 2010 must be born between January 1st and December 31st in 2003. The following are two types of school-age children who can both enter the school: the children who were born either in January or February of 2003 but postponed their admission, and children born in 2004 who wish to enter school early.

School parents whose child is either a year younger or older than the school age have a right to send him or her to school without the screening of the school principal, so the parents should take cautious steps before making the admission decision.

If any school parents wish to have an early admission or postpone the admission, they need to report it to a local community center either to approve or cancel the school admission.

1. School admission notice

You may receive a school admission notice either late January or early February. The school admission notice is a reminder that you have a school- age child(6 years old in Western age). Once the admission to school is approved, the eup, myeon or district office in its jurisdiction send the school admission notice to the families with a school-age child, which shows the admitted school, and dates for the school tour day and the admission ceremony.

If you do not receive the school admission notice within the period, please be sure to check it with the eup, myeon or district office in its jurisdiction. The received admission notice should be well kept and please present it to the school on the school tour day.

Moreover, if you receive the school admission notice, make sure to write down the important days such as the new students' school tour day around February 10th and the admission ceremony in early March, so that you do not miss those important days for your child.

취 학 통 지 서

발행번호: 호

주 소	OO시 OO동 112번지 OO아파트 OO동 OO호
보호자성명	
취학아동성명	
주민등록번호	
취학학교	OO초등학교
예비소집일시	****. 01. 21 14:00
입 학 일 시	****. 03. 02 11:00
등 록 기 간	

위 아동은 초·중등 교육법 제13조에 의하여 아래 학교에 배정되었사오니 소정 일시에 등교 취학시키시기 바랍니다.

20**년 12월 **일

OOOO장 (인)

School Admission Notice

Issue number:

Address	OOcity, OODong, 112Bunjee OOApt. OODong OOHo
Name of Guardian	
Name of the child	
Resident Registration Number	
Admission School	OO Elementary School
Orientation Date	****. 01. 21 14:00
Starting date of School	****. 03. 02 11:00
Registration Period	

Abovementioned child is assigned to the school above according to Article 13 of the primary and secondary school education law, so please admit your child to the assigned school on the starting date.

20**Year 12 Month **date

OOOO Principal (Stamp)

2. 취학 유예

초등학교에 입학할 연령이 되었지만 아동이 또래보다 몸이 왜소하거나 발달이 더딘 경우에는 취학 유예를 고려할 수도 있습니다. 취학을 유예하려면 보호자는 사유를 증명할 수 있는 서류(진단서 등)와 함께 취학 유예 신청서를 취학 예정 학교장에게 제출해 취학 유예 허가를 받아야 합니다. 그리고 취학 유예 결정을 받으면 주민자치센터에도 반드시 알려야 합니다.

유예 기간은 1년이며 특별한 이유가 있을 때에는 재차 유예할 수 있습니다.

3. 조기 입학

자녀를 조기 입학 시키려면 관할 교육청이나 인근 학교에 자녀가 입학할 수 있는지 문의해야 합니다. 준비할 서류는 조기입학 신청서와 주민등록등본이며 신청서는 학교에 준비되어 있습니다. 교육청과 학교는 보호자의 조기 입학 희망 의사를 확인한 뒤 아이가 초등학교 교과과정을 수용할 수 있는지에 대한 간단한 면접 등을 거쳐 생년월일 순으로 입학을 허용하게 됩니다.

조기 입학이 확정되고 난 후에는 자녀 앞에서 부모가 걱정하는 태도를 보여서는 안 됩니다. '너는 나이는 어리지만 학교에 가서 공부 할 자격이 있어.' 라는 말을 자주 해 주어서 자녀가 자신감을 가질 수 있도록 해야 합니다.

4. 신입생 예비소집

입학식 이전에 치르는 신입생 예비 소집이 이루어지며 가입학식이라고도 합니다. 입학 전에 취학 아동을 확인하고 학부모와 학생이 알아야 할 유의 사항을 전달하는 행사입니다. 하지만 공식적인 행사가 있는 것은 아니며, 취학 통지서를 제출한 다음 유인물을 받고 자녀와 함께 학교를 둘러보는 정도입니다.

예비소집일에 학교에 가서 먼저 동별로 마련된 접수창구에 취학통지서를 내고 성별, 오자, 탈자 등을 확인 받고 유인물을 받습니다.

이 유인물에는 학교장의 인사말, 교훈, 교가 · 교표 · 교목 · 교화 등 소개, 학교 연혁 소개, 입학식 안내, 입학 초기의 가정 지도 및 학부모 유의사항, 입학 후 학교생활 안내 등이 간략하게 적혀 있습니다. 이 날은 학교 배치도를 보고 자녀와 함께 학교 운동장과 자녀가 공부하게 될 1학년 교실, 특별실, 화장실 등을 둘러보는 것이 좋습니다.

2. Admission postponement

In the case of a runty or physically less developed child, the child can consider postponing the school admission regardless of his or her age. The admission postponement can only be accepted upon the submission of written diagnosis of the child and the application for the postponement to the principal to be.

3. Early admission

For the early admission of the child, the parents need to inquire for the admission details at a local education authority or nearby schools. The documents required are the application for early admission and a copy of the resident registration. The application for early admission can be picked up at a nearby elementary school. The children can be accepted to a school after a brief interview on their ability to take the elementary school curriculum in the order of their birthdays upon the admission wishes of their legal guardians which are confirmed by the local education authority and the related school.

The parents should not exhibit any worrisome attitude in front of the child after the confirmation of the admission. The child should be empowered by encouragements like " Although you are young, I know you can do it!"

4. School tour day

The school tour day prior to the admission ceremony day is called, "Gaiphawksik." This is an event for the school to inspect the children and address a few things that the children and their parents should be aware of. However, this is not an official school event, this is like taking a quick tour around the school with your kids after receiving the admission notice.

On the school tour day you simply need to show up at the reception desk, which is lined according to the different "Dongs," to submit the admission notice, check any misspellings, omitted words or letters on the related documents, and to receive the school information hand-outs.

The hand-outs include the greeting of the principal, along with general introduction such as school motto, school song, school symbol, school tree, school flower, school history, upcoming admission ceremony, things to be aware of for school parents, and brief description of the school life for their children following the admission. This is a perfect day for the children and the parents to take a quick tour around the school ground, the first graders' classrooms, special rooms, and bathrooms.

5. 입학식과 반 배정

입학식 날 정해진 시간 내에(예비소집시 확인) 아동과 학부모가 학교에 도착해서 아동의 반 배정 표를 확인 한 후 반 팻말 앞에 서 있으면 담임선생님이 나옵니다. 담임선생님은 한 사람씩 반가운 인사를 나누고 아동들에게 이름표를 달아 주며 출석을 확인합니다. 이 때 선생님이 자기 이름을 부르면 "예"하고 크게 대답할 수 있도록 부모가 미리 집에서 아동을 지도해 줘야 합니다.

입학식 순서는 국민의례, 입학 허가 선언, 교장 선생님의 환영 인사와 함께 간단한 당부의 말을 전합니다. 식이 끝나면 각 반마다 담임선생님의 인사가 이어지고 여러 가지 주의 사항을 알려 줍니다. 그리고 담임선생님은 학부모들에게 주간 학습 계획표와 함께 가정환경 조사서를 나눠 주고 아동들을 귀가 시킵니다.

반 배정은 학교마다 조금씩 다르지만 성별, 주거지별, 생년월일, 이름순서 등이 기준이 되며, 다양한 구성원을 고루 배치한다는 것입니다.

반 배정의 발표는 학교마다 다르지만 보통 예비 소집이 끝나고 아동들의 취학 확인이 끝나는 2월 말경에 발표가 됩니다. 대부분 입학식 당일에 배정된 반을 알려 주고 담임선생님을 소개하는데, 학교에 따라 홈페이지나 우편물을 통해 미리 알려 주기도 합니다.

6. 입학 전 건강 확인

입학하면서 학생 건강 기록부에 기록해야 할 항목들이 많이 있습니다.

학생 건강 기록부에는 취학 전 소아마비, 디프테리아, 파상풍, 백일해, 홍역 결핵, B형 간염, 일본뇌염 등의 접종 여부를 반드시 기록하게 되어 있습니다.

초등학교에 입학할 아이들은 새로운 학교생활에 적응하느라 신체적으로 큰 부담이 됩니다. 따라서 부모들은 아이들이 성공적인 학교생활을 보낼 수 있도록 사전에 준비를 해야 합니다.

1) 취학 전에 반드시 마쳐야 할 예방 접종

소아마비 2차 추가 접종과 DPT(디프테리아, 백일해, 파상풍)접종을 완료해야 합니다. 또한 BCG, B형 간염, MMR(홍역, 볼거리, 풍진), 일본 뇌염 등의 예방접종도 받아야 합니다.

2) 취학 전 해야 할 건강검진

부모들은 취학 전에 우리 아이들이 학교에 대해서 얼마나 많은 스트레스를 받고 있는지, 학습에 장애가 되는 정서적인 문제는 없는지, 시력이나 면역력 등 신체에 이상이 없는지 꼼꼼히 살펴보아야 합니다. 특히, 시력과 청력 검사는 필수이며 정기적인 치과 검진을 통해 영구치가 잘 나고 있는지, 충치는 없는지 살펴봅니다. 또, 아이들의 집중력을 떨어뜨릴 수 있는 축농증은 취학 전 치료가 필요합니다.

5. Admission ceremony and assigning classes

On the day of the admission ceremony, which was specified on the school tour day, the child and the parents arrive at school and check the chart showing the class assigned to their child, and wait in front of the sign, then the homeroom teacher shows up. The homeroom teacher cheerfully greets the children one at a time, and call the roll as he or she attaches the name tag on the chest of each child. You should have your child practice answering the call by "Yea," at home, so your child can answer it aloud and clear in the class.

The admission ceremony starts in the order of the pledge of allegiance, the announcement of the admission approval, welcoming address by the principal, and passing along a few requests, which are often followed by a greeting and comments by a homeroom teacher in their assigned classrooms. Then the children are sent home upon receiving the weekly lesson plans and having completed the family background report form.

Assigning class is mostly based on sex, home location, birthday, and name although it is slightly different from school to school; consequently, the students can be evenly assigned to the classes.

The announcement of the assigned class is a little different depending on the school, but the announcement is usually followed by the school tour day around the end of February, which is near the end of the admission confirmation process. The assigned class and the homeroom teacher are announced on the school ceremony day, but some school announce them beforehand by e-mail or regular mail.

6. Health check-up prior to the admission

There are many health items that need to be recorded on the students' health record. The following vaccinations must be recorded on the students' health record prior to the admission: polio, diphtheria, tetanus, pertussis, measles, tuberculous, hepatitis B, and Japanese encephalitis.

Many new students physically go under lots of stress as they adapt to a new school life. Therefore, parents should help their child prepare for a successful school life in advance.

1) The vaccinations that must be completed prior to the admission

The 2nd polio vaccination and DPT(diphtheria, pertussis, tetanus) vaccinations must be completed. Moreover, BCG, hepatitis B, MMR(measles, mumps, rubella) and Japanese encephalitis vaccinations must be completed as well.

2) Health check-up prior to the admission

The parents need to pay close attention to the amount of stress their children might be under because of school, or any emotional problems leading to learning difficulties, or any physical problems such as vision, or the level of immunity. It is extremely important to point out that the prior vision and hearing tests are prerequisite, and make sure that they have no cavities and their permanent teeth are in place. Moreover, the sinus infection, which can lower the child's concentration level, needs to be treated.

7. 취학준비물

취학준비물을 구입할 때에는 예비소집 때 나누어 주는 안내문과 입학 후 배부되는 주간 학습 계획표를 참고하는 것이 좋습니다. 입학 후 한 달간의 학교적응기간에 준비해도 늦지 않으며 준비하고자 한다면 먼저 나름대로 필요한 목록과 수량을 정해야 합니다. 준비물을 구입 할 때는 아동과 함께 다니면서 챙기는 것도 자녀 교육의 한 방법이며, 아동이 가지고 다녀야 할 모든 물건에는 반드시 이름을 써야 합니다. 교과서, 공책은 물론이고 연필, 색연필, 크레파스, 등은 낱개마다 이름을 써 붙이는 것이 좋습니다. 가방, 자. 지우개, 실내화, 운동화, 열쇠, 악기, 우산 등에도 유성 팬이나 견출지를 이용해 이름을 쓰도록 합니다. 이때 책임감을 길러 주기 위해 아동 스스로 자신의 이름을 써서 붙이게 하는 것이 좋습니다.

1) 책가방

책가방은 무엇보다 아동들이 들고 다니기에 가볍고 편해야하며 튼튼한 것을 골라야 합니다. 어깨 끈이 제대로 박음질 되어 있는지 확인하고 바닥에 닿는 부분의 마감처리가 잘 되어 있는 것과 통풍이 잘 되는 소재와 비 오는 날을 대비해 방수 처리가 되어 있고 눈에 잘 띄는 밝은 색을 고를 필요가 있습니다. 바퀴가 달린 책가방도 좋으며, 책, 공책, 필통이 충분히 들어갈 만한 크기로 A4파일 정도의 높이가 되면 적당합니다. 디자인이 복잡하거나 장식이 많은 것은 금물, 등받이가 있어서 책상 옆에 세워 놓아도 넘어지지 않는 것이 좋습니다. 가방에 나뉘는 칸은 작은 문구류와 소지품을 넣을 수 있는 여분의 분리 공간이 있고 외부에 작은 주머니가 있으면 좋습니다.

2) 신발

신발은 가볍고 신고 벗기에 편한 것이 좋으며 실내에서 신는 하얀 실내화도 필요합니다. 신발은 양말을 신은 상태에서 불편하지 않게 꼭 맞는 것을 고르는 게 좋습니다. 조금 더 오래 신기려고 큰 신발을 사 주면 뛰다가 넘어지기 쉽습니다. 어차피 일 년에 2~4개의 신발을 사용하기 때문에 미리 두 개를 구입하여 교대로 신기는 것도 요령입니다. 신발을 번갈아 신게 하면 조금은 더 오래 깨끗하게 신을 수 있습니다.

3) 신발주머니

책가방과 세트로 나온 것을 그대로 쓰셔도 괜찮습니다. 아이가 조금 불편해하면 근처 문구점에서 1,000원~3,000원대의 주머니 형 신발주머니를 따로 구입하셔도 됩니다. 신발장이 있는 학교는 준비 하지 않아도 되므로 미리 알아보고 구입해야 합니다.

7. School supplies for starting school

It would be better for the parents to refer to the instruction hand-out and the weekly lesson plans handed out to them on the school tour day when purchasing the school supplies. Actually, it wouldn't be that late to start getting the supplies during the month of adaptation period after the school start. When you get the school supplies, you need to decide on the needed items and the quantity. When getting them, accompanying your child can be one of the educational experiences for your child, and be sure to write down the name on every item purchased. Therefore, it would be better to write down the name of your child not just on the textbooks and notebooks but also on every school supply such as the pencils, colored pencils, and crayons. Oil pens or plastic taps are recommended to write the name with on the schoolbag, ruler, eraser, indoor sandals, sneakers, keys, musical instruments, and umbrella. It is also recommended that the child should write his name down and attach labels for himself to foster a sense of responsibility.

1) Schoolbag

You need to select a durable schoolbag that is comfortable and light enough to carry around. The shoulder strap should have a backstitch, and the rubbing bottom part needs to have an adequate bottom finish; moreover, it should be made of bright ventilated waterproof material for a rainy day. A schoolbag with wheels is also good, and the one with A4 file height, which is enough to fit books, notebooks, and a pencil case, is just as adequate. One with a complex design or too much decoration should be avoided, and it is also recommended to get a bag with a back support that resists falling when left stand next to a desk. It would be even better if the bag has extra separated rooms in it with a small extra bag on the outside.

2) Shoes

It is nice to have a pair of shoes that is light and comfortable enough to easily put on and take off. A pair of white sandals used for indoor is also needed. The shoes that adequately fit without causing any discomforts should be selected. Purchasing big shoes for longer use can easily cause a trip and fall while running. In any case, a child uses average 2 or 4 pairs of shoes a year, so it would be smart to get 2 pairs of shoes beforehand and alternate them. When your child wears the shoes alternately, they can wear them cleaner for longer time.

3) Shoes bag

It is okay to use the bag that comes with the shoes. If it is not convenient for the child, one with 1,000 to 3,000 won price range can be purchased at a local stationery store. The students who go to a school equipped with a shoe cabinets do not have to get it.

4) 연필

아이가 아무리 글씨를 잘 쓰려고 해도 잘 쓰기 어려운 단계입니다. HB 보다는 부드러운 2B 연필이 좋습니다. 샤프나 볼펜은 바른 글씨체를 정착시키는 데 도움이 되지 않기 때문에 준바하지 않는 것이 좋습니다. 요즘 아이들이 컴퓨터를 많이 하다 보니 글씨를 잘 쓰는 아이들을 찾는 게 힘들 정도입니다. 글씨를 잘 못 쓴다고 해서 굳이 야단을 칠 필요는 없습니다. 다른 집 아이들도 거의 비슷하기 때문입니다. 연필은 다섯 자루 이상을 잘 깎아 필통에 넣어 주시기 바랍니다. 글씨를 쓰다가 장난을 치면 심이 부러질 수 있고 친구의 칼을 빌려 스스로 깎아 보려고 하다가 손을 다치는 경우가 생깁니다. 미리 충분할 만큼 준비하여 필통에 넣어 주는 게 좋습니다.

5) 필통

요즘 학교에서는 철제 필통은 금기시 되고 있습니다. 떨어뜨리면 요란한 소리가 나면서 안의 내용물이 사방으로 흩어져 면학분위기를 어지럽히기 때문입니다. 골고루 넣을 수 있고 흔들릴 때 소리가 나지 않는 헝겊 필통 류가 좋습니다. 처음부터 비싼 필통을 사주기보다는 차라리 쓰기 편한 헝겊 필통에 연필꽂이까지 있는 것을 사 주는 것이 좋습니다.

6) 책받침

요즘에는 책받침을 판매하지 않는 문구점이 많이 있습니다. 오래전에는 노트의 질이 좋지 않아 아이들이 힘을 주어 글씨를 쓰거나 지우개를 지울 때 찢어지는 경우가 많았지만 지금은 굳이 책받침을 대지 않아도 글씨를 쓸 때 아무 지장이 없습니다. 다만 아이가 유난히 손에 힘을 주고 쓴다면 예쁜 그림이 들어 있는 것을 코팅하여 쓰면 됩니다.

7) 지우개

색소가 첨가되지 않은 지우개가 잘 지워지므로 아무 색깔이나 무늬가 없는 것이 좋으며 공책이 찢어지지 않을 정도의 부드러운 것이 좋습니다. 비싼 지우개는 아이가 쉽게 잃어버리는 경우가 있기 때문에 평범한 것이 좋습니다.

8) 가위

가위는 날이 ㄱ자로 꺾여 있는 '안전가위'를 사주는 것이 좋습니다. 비닐류가 잘 오려지지 않는 단점은 있지만 초등 1학년은 주로 색종이를 자르기 때문에 문제가 없습니다. 안전가위는 아이들이 장난을 치더라도 다칠 염려가 별로 없기 때문에 아주 중요합니다. 왼손잡이 아이의 경우 왼손잡이 가위를 사 주는 게 좋습니다. 일부 브랜드에서 소량만 생산을 하기 때문에 구매하는 데 어려움이 따를 수도 있습니다. 하지만 집 근처 문구점에 부탁을 해 놓으면 구해 줄 것입니다. 왼손잡이 가위가 필요한 이유는 일반 가위를 왼손으로 쓰게 되면 색종이나 도화지의 잘리는 절단면이 가려 제대로 보이지 않기 때문에 곧게 자를 수 없어서입니다. 윗날과 아랫날의 위치가 반대로 되어 있습니다. 칼은 사주지 않아도 됩니다. 웬만한 것은 가위로 다 자를 수 있고 연필은 집에서 부모님께서 깎아 주시면 됩니다.

4) Pencils

Children are still in a period that no matter how hard they try to write well, it is still hard for them to do so. Soft 2B pencils are preferred over HB. Since both mechanical pencils and ball-pointed pens do not help improve students' handwriting, there is no need to get one. Since many children use a computer to write, so it is hard to find children who write well. You do not need to scold them because they have a sloppy handwriting. Most kids have the same problem. More than five pencils need to be well sharpened and placed in a pencil case. Children often break the pencil lead while playing with it, or they cut their hands while sharpening it for themselves with their friend's knife. It would be better to prepare enough pencils beforehand and place them in their pencil case.

5) Pencil case

Iron pencil cases have been prohibited at school these days because they often accompany loud noise when falling and disturb the academic atmosphere. Pencil cases made of flexible and noiseless cloth that can evenly keep things are much better to have. It would be better to buy your child a cloth pencil case with pencil holders rather than getting them an expensive one from the start.

6) Plastic sheet to rest writing paper on

Many stationery stores have stopped selling the plastic sheets nowadays. The quality of paper once used for notebooks was not that good, so it was often torn or ripped when the children pressed it hard to write on the notebooks. However, there has not been any more problem with the paper when writing on it without the plastic sheet under. If your child tends to write it hard against the notebook, getting him a plastic sheet with a coated cute picture would be a good idea.

7) Eraser

Erasers without any artificial color added work the best, so it would be better to get a soft one without any colors or designs on it. Children tend to lose an expensive one so easily, so getting him a regular one is better.

8) Scissors

Purchasing a safe scissor with a ㄱ shape is better. The safe scissor has a problem cutting vinyl materials. However, first graders mostly cut colored papers with it, so there wouldn't be any problems. Having safe scissors around is important because it keeps children safe even from playing with them. Getting left hander, left-handed scissors are also an idea. However, getting left-handed scissors are not always easy, because most stores usually carry only a few in stock. You can put it on order through a nearby stationery store. Left-handed scissors are needed because the cutting section of the colored or drawing papers is often hidden; therefore, the paper cannot be cut straight if regular scissors are used. The upper and lower edges are inversely aligned. There is no need to buy them a knife. Most of things can be easily cut by a knife, and you can sharpen the pencils for them at home.

9) 자

자는 20cm 정도가 공책 사이즈와 맞아 아이들이 쓰기에 적당합니다.

10) 종합장과 스케치북

종합장과 스케치북은 정말 많이 쓰게 됩니다. 그렇다고 해서 잔뜩 한꺼번에 사다 놓는 것은 결코 좋지 않습니다. 그림이 다양하지 않아 아이가 식상해 하는 경우가 있고 유행하는 캐릭터의 제품이 나오면 또 그것을 사고 싶어 하기 때문입니다. 때로는 직접 사오도록 하여 스스로 제품을 고르는 안목과 경제관념을 심어 주는 것도 좋기 때문입니다. 유선 종합장 보다는 무선 종합장을 훨씬 많이 쓰게 됩니다.

11) 일기장

일기장은 A4 사이즈의 그림일기장을 사 주는 게 좋습니다. 몇 년 전 까지는 스케치북형 그림일기가 주를 이뤘지만 아이들 가방에 들어가지 않아 휴대가 불편하고 비가 오는 날이면 아이들의 고생이 커지는 경우가 있기 때문에 가방에 쏙 들어가는 A4 사이즈의 그림일기를 권하는 것입니다. 제품을 잘 보고 왼쪽에 그림, 오른쪽에 글씨를 쓸 수 있는지 확인하고 구입하시기 바랍니다. 가끔 앞면에 그림 뒷면에 글씨를 쓰는 제품이 있는데 이럴 때는 그림의 내용과 일기의 내용이 한 눈에 들어오지 않기 때문에 아주 불편합니다. 일반적으로 1학기가 끝나갈 때쯤 선생님이 가져오라고 하여 그림일기를 가르치면서 쓰게 하는 경우가 많지만 학기 초부터 준비물로 들어가는 경우도 가끔 있습니다. 학교에서 나눠 준 가정 통신문을 잘 참고하시면 됩니다. 노트 식으로 되어 있는 그림일기의 경우 그림을 그릴 수 있는 공간이 너무 적어 아이가 성의 없는 그림일기를 쓸 확률이 높습니다.

12) 색연필

색연필은 종이로 풀어 쓰는 것보다는 돌리는 색연필이 좋습니다. 종이로 된 색연필은 외부 압력에 잘 부러져 가방 안에서 이리저리 엉망이 되기 쉽습니다. 일반적인 제품은 12색이지만 아이가 그림 그리기를 좋아 한다거나 하면 금색, 은색 등이 들어 있는 색이 많은 색연필을 사 주는 것도 좋습니다.

13) 크레파스

크레파스는 주로 24색을 쓰지만 학교에서 18색을 원하는 경우도 있습니다. 미술 시간에 선생님이 지시하는 색과 아이들이 인지하는 색이 모두 같아야 가르치기 쉽기 때문에 다양한 색이 들어 있는 것은 오히려 좋지 않은 경우가 있습니다. 몇 색인지 지정되어 있는 경우가 많으니 '주간학습계획표'나 '알림장'을 참고하시면 됩니다.

9) Rulers

A 20cm ruler is equivalent to a size of notebook, so it is just adequate for children.

10) Exercise notebooks and Sketchbooks

Scribble pads and Sketchbooks are used a lot. However, purchasing too many of them at once is not a good idea. Children may become displeased about the fact that the scribble pads and Sketchbooks may not have diverse pictures on them; moreover, they may find other up-to-date and trendy ones much more attractive and eventually want to buy them. Letting them choose the ones that they want for themselves can actually help them get discerning eyes and a sense of economy. Lineless exercise notebooks are much more commonly used than the lined ones.

11) Diary

It is a good idea to buy a A4 size picture diary. The A4 size illustrated diary which fits perfectly into the schoolbag is now recommended. Until a couple years ago a sketchbook styled picture diary was used, but it is no longer in use because it was too big to fit into a schoolbag and not portable enough to carry around. Check out the product thoroughly before purchasing it, and make sure it has a picture on the left, and the writing space on the right. On and off you may come across with a diary that has a picture printed on the front and the writing space on the back of the sheet. This kind of diary is very uncomfortable because the two are overlapped and hard to see it clearly. Most likely the students do not learn or start writing the picture diary until the end of the first semester, but in other cases, they start to learn and write it as early as the beginning of the first semester. Make sure to thoroughly read the school newsletter. The notebook styled picture diaries do not have enough space for drawing pictures, so children, more often than not, end up writing the diary insincerely.

12) Colored pencils

The colored pencils that revolve are better than the ones that need to be unwrapped. The colored pencils wrapped around by paper can easily be broken by external pressure and make quite a mess inside the schoolbag. Generally, there are 12 different colors. However, if your child likes to draw pictures a lot, it will be better to get a pencil set with lots of different colors including gold, and silver.

13) Crayons

Crayons usually have 24 different colors, but schools sometimes want ones with only 18 different colors. It will be easier for the teacher to teach the colors when the color related lessons taught in the art class are corresponded with the colors that the children perceive; therefore, it would not be such a good idea to get the ones with too many colors. The number of the colors is often set by the school, so please read the 'Weekly Lesson Plans" or "School Announcement."

14) 악기류

아이들이 초등과정에서 준비해야 하는 악기는 리코더, 리듬악기 세트, 멜로디언, 소고, 실로폰 등이 있습니다. 캐스터네츠나 트라이앵글, 탬버린 등은 모두 리듬악기 세트에 들어 있으니 그것을 사 주시면 됩니다. 유치원 졸업선물로 각광을 받고 있기 때문에 선물로 받은 것이 있다면 교과 과정에 따라 필요한 것을 하나씩 빼 주거나 하면 됩니다.

15) 우산

저학년의 경우 우산은 긴 우산(장우산)이 좋습니다. 아이들이 펼쳤다가 다시 접는 게 편리하고 우산을 접은 상태에서 들고 다녀도 눈에 잘 띄고 분실의 우려도 적기 때문입니다. 접는 우산의 경우 펼치기는 쉽지만 아이들이 접는 게 쉽지 않습니다. 특이한 우산보다는 그냥 단순하고 밝은 색의 우산이 좋습니다.

16) 공책(노트)

1학년의 경우 처음에는 쓰기8칸(단어용) 공책, 조금 지나면 쓰기10칸(문장용) 공책을 사용하며 2학기에는 줄 공책을 사용합니다. 그러므로 미리 많이 준비하지 말고 학교에서 요구할 때 구입하는 것이 좋습니다. 그밖에 알림장, 종합장, 받아쓰기 공책 등이 필요하며 학교에 따라 영어 노트가 필요한 경우도 있습니다. 거의 많은 수업을 종합장으로 다 할 수 있기 때문에 공책이 많이 필요하지는 않습니다. 여름 방학쯤에 관찰기록장이나 독서록이 필요한 경우도 있습니다. 따라서 노트는 선물용 '노트세트'를 구입 할 필요는 없습니다. 선생님에 따라 '몇 줄 노트' 식으로 줄을 지정 해 주는 경우도 있습니다.

17) 연필깎이

연필깎이는 튼튼한 것을 사 주는 게 좋습니다. 주의해야 할 것은 미술연필이나 나무 색연필 등은 절대로 깎지 마셔야 한다는 점입니다. 생산 기준에 따라 HB연필을 기준으로 생산하기 때문에 심이 무른 4B 연필이나 나무 색연필을 깎게 되면 칼날이 돌아가는 힘을 버티지 못하고 연필깎이 안에서 심이 부러지게 됩니다.

14) Musical instruments

The following are the musical instruments the children need to prepare: recorder, rhythmic instruments set, melodion, a tabor, and a xylophone. Castanets, triangle, tambourine are all included in a rhythmic instruments set, so just buy him the set. The rhythmic instruments set is a popular kindergarten graduation gift, so, sometimes, you do not have to get one separately. If you have one, just use them one at a time as needed.

15) Umbrella

It would be better for the lower grades get a long umbrella, because it is convenient for the children to open and fold it, it easily catches people's eyes when it is carried around as folded, and less likely to lose it. The retractable umbrellas are easier for the children to open it than to fold it. A simple and bright umbrella is better than an odd one.

16) Notebook

First graders use 8 lined notebook(for words), later move onto 10 lined notebook(for sentences). Second graders use regularly lined notebooks. Therefore, you do not need to get a lot of them in advance, just get one as needed when school asks you to. Besides, a school announcement, an exercise notebook, and a dictation notebook are also needed, and some school require an separate English notebook. An exercise notebook can be used in just about all classes, so you do not need that many notebooks. An watch log or booklist are also needed at around summer vacation. So, purchasing a notebook set is not always a good idea, The number of the lines varies depending on the teacher.

17) Pencil sharpener

Buy your child a strong pencil sharpener. Keep in mind never to sharpen an art pencil or a colored pencil. Most of the sharpeners are designed to sharpen HB pencils. Therefore, if you try to sharpen the 4B pencils, the soft pencil lead cannot take the force of the blade, and it breaks.

18) 물 티슈

학교에서 미술시간에 찰흙 등으로 수업을 하거나 물감으로 그림을 그리다 보면 이곳 저곳에 묻는 경우가 많습니다. 물 티슈를 넣어 주면 아이가 슬기롭게 대처할 수 있게 됩니다. 준비물로 물수건을 가져오라고 할 때는 물 티슈와 더불어 '케이스 타월'이라는 제품을 함께 들려 보내시면 됩니다. 케이스 타월이라는 제품은 손바닥만 한 타월과 케이스가 함께 있어 아이들이 타월을 사용 한 후에 젖은 채로 케이스에 담아 책가방에 넣을 수 있기 때문입니다.

19) 색종이

색종이도 많이 쓰는 종류에 해당합니다. 낱장으로 그때그때 구입하기에는 번거롭기 때문에 한 통을 사 놓는 것이 좋습니다.

20) 붓 세트

붓 세트도 케이스가 있는 것을 구입하는 게 좋습니다.

21) 물감

물감은 플라스틱 케이스에 들어 있는 것을 권하고 싶습니다. 똑딱이가 달린 물감을 사주면 물감이 흐르는 것을 예방을 할 수 있습니다.

22) 사인펜

많이 사용하지는 않지만 꼭 쓰게 되는 제품입니다. 아이들이 쓰기에는 크레파스나 색연필보다 더 편리하고 그림일기를 쓰거나 자신만의 다이어리를 예쁘게 꾸밀 때도 씁니다. 사인펜을 구입할 때는 제조연도를 꼭 확인하시기 바라고 1년 이내의 제품을 사 주는 게 좋습니다.

그 외에도 황화일, 끌리어 파일, 파일케이스, 사물함바구니, 사물함열쇠, 치약칫솔세트, 바둑돌, 고무찰흙, 사포, 학 종이, 시트지 등이 필요 합니다.

18) Wet tissue

The classroom gets pretty messy here and there as the students work with clay or paint with watercolor in an art class. If you leave wet tissue in the schoolbag, your child can use it wisely. When the wet tissue is asked for, it is better to bring a "Case towel" with it. Case towel refers to a palm-size towel that comes with its case. The wet towel can be kept in the case and put it in a schoolbag after they finish using it.

19) Colored paper

Colored papers are one of the most frequently used types of school supplies. Purchasing a piece of paper each time can be cumbersome. It is definitely better to buy a sheaf of papers for future use.

20) Brush Set

Getting a brush set that comes with a case is better.

21) Paints

Paints that come in a case is recommended. Getting the paints with a cap can prevent the paints from leaking.

22) Magic Markers

It is not used so often, but you will have to use it eventually. It is more convenient than crayons or colored pencils, and it comes very handy when writing a picture diary or decorating a diary. It is smart to check the manufacturing date and get the one less than a year old.

Moreover, they will need yellow file folders, clear file folders, a file case, a personal basket, the locker key, a toothpaste and toothbrush set, stone checkers, rubber clay, sandpapers, papers for folding, and paper sheets.

취학 전 길러줘야 할 생활 습관

입학을 앞둔 학부모도 스트레스를 받지만 아이도 알게 모르게 심리적 스트레스를 받습니다. 입학 전에 가장 주의해야 할 점은 어린이에게 무리한 심리적 부담을 주지 말아야 한다는 것입니다. 입학을 앞둔 6~7세의 어린이들은 학교에 대한 두려움을 가지고 있습니다. 가정이라는 울타리를 벗어나 새로운 환경에 들어가는 데 대해 부담을 갖지 않도록 심리적 안정을 찾도록 해야 합니다. 학교란 선생님과 새로운 친구를 만나 재미있게 공부하고 생활하는 곳이라는 점을 일깨워 빨리 학교에 가고 싶다는 생각을 갖도록 해주는 것이 최선의 방법입니다.

1. 일찍 일어나기

아이가 학교에 가면 부모님들이 제일 먼저, 또 제일 많이 걱정하고 신경을 쓰는 부분이 지각하지 않게 하는 것입니다. 아침이 정신없으면 종일 어수선하게 마련입니다. 초등학교의 등교시간은 유치원보다 빠르기 때문에 등교시간에 허둥대지 않도록 저녁에 일찍 자고, 늦어도 등교하기 1시간 전에 일어나는 습관을 들입니다. 또 아침에 일어나는 시간과 저녁에 TV 보는 시간을 아이와 함께 정하고 그것을 꾸준히 지키도록 도와주며, 학교는 매일 정해진 시간에 맞춰서 가야 하는 곳이라고 설명해줍니다.

등교시간은 8시 30분에서 50분 사이에 이루어지므로 아침식사와 용변까지 마무리하기 위해서는 7시에서 7시 30분 사이에 일어나는 연습을 시켜야 합니다. 낮잠을 자던 버릇이 있는 아이들은 수업시간에 조는 경우가 있으므로 낮잠은 되도록 자지 않는 것이 좋으며 또 학교에 늦지 않는 것도 중요하지만, 너무 일찍 가는 것도 피해야 합니다. 교실 문을 열어두지 않거나 선생님이 교실에 있지 않다면 안전사고의 위험이 있기 때문입니다.

밤에는 아이의 성장을 돕는 호르몬이 밤 10시에서 새벽 2시 사이에 활발하게 분비되므로 밤에는 9시 30분경에 잠자리에 들어 숙면을 취할 수 있도록 지도를 하여야 학습의 기본인 기억력을 향상시키는데 도움이 됩니다. 아이가 잠잘 시간이 되면 아이 방에 가서 책을 읽어주며 잠이 들도록 유도하고 편한 잠을 잘 수 있도록 조용한 분위기를 만들어 주어야 합니다. 아이가 같은 시간대에 잠이 드는 습관을 가질 때 까지 가족 모두가 아이의 생활 패턴에 맞추는 노력이 필요합니다.

The Types of Lifestyle Their Child Should Have Before Entering School

Not only the school parents facing the upcoming admission go under stress but also the child is most likely to experiences some degree of psychological stress as well. It is important to note that the parents should not impose a great deal of psychological stress on the child. Children of 6 to 7 years old tend to fear school. The parents should search for ways to comfort their children burdened by moving away from the home boundary into a new environment. The best way is perhaps making them want to go to school by reminding them that school is a place to start an interesting life by meeting teachers and new friends.

1. Getting up early

The foremost concern of the parents is making sure their child is not late for school. If you are swamped in the morning, you will be in a muddle all day. It would be a good habit to go to sleep early in the evening and wake up about an hour early before school starts because all elementary schools start earlier than kindergartens in the morning. If your child does not get up early in the morning, he or she will be flustered. Setting the wake-up call and the T.V. viewing time in the evening with your child, and helping them comply with the rules are very important because they consistently have to go to school at a certain time.

The children usually go to school between 8:30 am and 8:50 am, so they need to practice getting up between 7:00 am and 7:30 am to use the bathroom and eat breakfast. A child with the habit of taking a nap often falls asleep in the class, if possible, it is better for him not to take a nap. Going to school either too early or late needs to be avoided. If the class door is left open without a teacher in the class, there will be a safety concern. There is active secretion of growth hormone among the children of that age between 10:00 pm to 2:00 am, so going to bed before 9:00 pm will enhance their memory capacity. When the bedtime is near, go to his or her room and read him a book and make a quiet atmosphere, so they can fall asleep easily and have a good night sleep. All family members need to fit their schedules into the child's until he or she becomes used to the new bedtime.

2. 바른 식습관 갖기

대부분의 학교에서는 1학년 아이들도 점심을 먹고 하교하는 경우가 많습니다. 하지만 편식이 심한 아이들은 급식에 적응하기 어렵기 때문에 가정에서 미리 지도해야 합니다. 또한 산만하거나 잘 흘리는 습관도 입학 전에 바로잡아야 합니다.

여러 가지 반찬을 골고루 먹기, 너무 많은 양을 한꺼번에 입에 넣지 말기, 입에 들어간 음식은 보이지 않게 입을 다물고 씹어 먹기, 밥 먹는 동안에는 돌아다니거나 뒤돌아보며 떠들지 않기, 젓가락 바른 자세로 잡기 등이 있습니다.

이러한 식사예절은 단시간에 익히기 어렵고 건강과 직결되는 문제이기 때문에 생활습관 중에서도 매우 중요합니다.

식사예절 중 골고루 먹는 것은 특히 강조할 만한데, 실제 음식을 앞에 두고 못 먹겠다고 엉엉 울거나, 배가 아프다고 하거나, 억지로 먹어 토하는 등 교사를 당혹스럽게 하는 경우가 종종 있습니다.

식사는 대략 30분 안에 마칠 수 있게 하고, 우유팩이나 요구르트 뚜껑을 따는 연습도 미리 해두면 좋습니다. 의외로 7세 아이 중에 기본적인 것도 하지 못하는 아이들이 많습니다.

또한 아침밥은 꼭 먹는 습관을 길러주십시오. 아침을 챙겨먹지 않으면 둘째 시간만 지나면 기운이 빠집니다. 1,2학년에는 체력이 약한 아이들이 많으므로 아침밥은 꼭 챙겨주시기 바랍니다.

3. 등하굣길 익히기

초등학생 교통사고는 1~2학년 때 가장 많이 일어납니다. 따라서 입학 전 등·하교 지도는 필수입니다. 아이와 함께 손을 잡고 집에서 학교까지 걸어가며 안전한 등·하굣길을 알려줍니다. 아이들은 등·하굣길에 친구들과 함께 다니면서 사회성을 기르게 됩니다.

쉬는 날 가족과 함께 학교를 한 바퀴 돌아보면서 어디에 무엇이 있나 살펴두면 입학해서도 아이가 낯설어 하지 않습니다. 학교 가는 길에 무엇이 있는지, 조심할 곳은 어디인지, 횡단보도는 어디에 있는지 등을 꼼꼼하게 살피고 학교 안의 1학년 교실, 화장실, 교무실의 위치도 익혀둡니다. 횡단보도 건너는 요령, 교차로 지날 때의 요령 등을 알려줍니다. 초등학교 입학 후 2.3 주간은 적응학습기간으로 수업이 일찍 끝나고, 한 달 정도는 교사가 등·하교 안전에 신경을 써줍니다. 하지만 결국 아이 혼자 등·하교를 해야 하므로 건널목 건너기 등에 특히 주의를 주고, 등하굣길에 문구점 앞에서 게임을 하거나 군것질을 하는 등 다른 곳에 정신을 빼앗기지 않게 합니다.

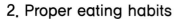

2. Proper eating habits

Most first graders go home after eating lunch. However, some picky eaters have hard time getting used to the school foods, so they often require guidance and practice that start at home. You must help them not to be distracted or drop their food. There are many inappropriate table manners that need to be corrected. The appropriate table manner are as follows: equally eating from all side dishes, not stuffing too much food into the mouth at once, chewing food with the mouth closed, not going around and making a fuss while eating, holding chopsticks in a proper manner. Since correct table manners are hard to master in a short period of time and directly linked with one's health, they are considered very important living habits.

Of the table manners, the importance of evenly eating all other foods is specially emphasized. Teachers are often baffled by students who refuse to eat the foods in front of them by crying out loud, complain of stomachache, and reluctantly eat and vomit.

Help them finish their meal approximately in half an hour, and have them practice taking off the caps of their milk packs and yogurt. Many 7 years old children have hard time simply doing very basic things like that.

Foster the habit of eating a very important meal of the day: breakfast. The children lose their strength after second class period if they skip breakfast. There are many physically weak first and second graders; therefore, be sure to have them eat breakfast.

3. Becoming familiar with the routes from and to school

Elementary students get into traffic accidents most frequently for the first 2 years. Thus, the thorough instructions on the routes from and to school is a must. You point out the safe routes to your child as you and your child walk hand in hand from home to school. As your child walks on the road from and to school with his friends, he or she learns how to socialize with them.

If you check out the school as you walk around it with your family on your day off, the child will not feel unease about the place when he or she enters the school. Checking out the places between home and school, remembering the dangerous spots, remembering exactly where the crosswalk is, and getting familiar with the locations of the classroom, bathrooms, and teacher's room are important places to know. Ways to cross the crosswalk, and intersections should be well instructed. The first 2 or 3 weeks is an adaptation period, so students get out of school early, and teachers help their students walk safely from and to school for about a month. However, your child will have to walk back and forth by himself, so you should help him not to get distracted on his way home. For instances, you should not let your child play the arcade games at a stationery store or snack on junkfood.

4. 공손한 인사예절

인사는 사회성의 기본입니다. 부모님, 선생님과 친구, 동네 어른들께 인사하는 습관을 길러줍니다.

"학교 다녀오겠습니다", "학교 다녀왔습니다", "반갑습니다", "고맙습니다", "죄송합니다", "미안해" 등 때와 장소, 대상, 상황에 맞추어 인사하는 법을 일러주고, 유아어에서 벗어나 존댓말 쓰기도 훈련시킵니다.

또한 어른께 물건을 드릴 때 두 손으로 공손히 드린다든지 하는 기본 예의범절도 알려줍니다.

공손한 인사와 자세는 교사와 친구 관계에도 영향을 미치는 만큼 꼭 신경을 써야합니다.

5. 사교성 키우기

처음 만난 친구들과 어울리려면 낯선 장소에 대한 두려움을 없애고 남을 배려하는 마음이 필요합니다. 놀이공원이나 박물관 등 아이가 좋아할 만한 장소로 데려가 다양한 경험을 쌓고 그곳에서 공공질서를 지키게 하면 좋은 훈련이 됩니다. 이웃이나 친척과 함께 가면 또래 친구들과 어울리면서 아이들끼리 지켜야 할 일도 자연스럽게 체험할 수 있습니다.

6. 물건 관리하기

지우개, 연필, 실내화주머니 등은 물론 교과서도 잃어버려 다시 사는 경우가 종종 있습니다. 엄마가 대신 물건을 정리해주고 관리해주는 습관 때문입니다.

각 학용품에 스스로 이름을 쓰고 물건을 사용한 뒤에는 반드시 제자리에 두는 습관을 들이게 합니다. 그러기 위해서는 아이가 느려도 참고 기다려주는 엄마의 자세가 필요합니다. 또한 잃어버렸다고 해서 무턱대고 다시 사주거나 잃어버릴 것을 대비해 대량으로 사두는 것은 바람직하지 않습니다.

왜 잃어버렸는지 스스로 잘못을 깨닫게 하는 것이 우선입니다.

또한 신발장에서 자신의 신발을 찾는 연습도 필요합니다.

4. Polite etiquette

Greeting is the foundation of all socialization. Foster the habit of greeting the parents, teachers and friends, and senior neighbors. Instruct your child to appropriately use the following language in their proper contexts such as "Hawk-Gyo-Da-Nyu-Oh-Get-Seum-Ni-Da," "Hawk-Gyo-Da-Nyu-Wat-Seum-Ni-Da," "Ban-Gap-Seum-Ni-Da," "Go-Map-Seum-Ni-Da," "Je-Seong-Ham-Ni-Da," and "Mi-Ahn-Hea." Moreover, have them step out of using childish words and languages, and train them to use honorific form of language. In addition, give your child lessons in etiquette such as handing out things politely with two hands to old people. Polite greetings and posture significantly affect the relationship with teachers and friends, so remind them to be more observant on those.

5. Fostering sociability

Children should not be afraid of new places and should be considerate of others' feelings to get along with people they just met. Taking your child to likeable places like a theme park or museum where your child can experience lots of things and teaching him or her to keep public order in those public places would be considered a great training. If your child goes there with his neighbors and relatives, he will learn how to mingle with his peers and their rules to keep the relationship going.

6. Keeping personal belongings

Children often lose erasers, pencils, a bag for indoor slippers, and textbooks, because it has been a mothers' responsibility to look after them. It would be an important habit for your child to write his own name down on each item, and put them away where they are supposed to be. Therefore, the mother has be patient with her child even if he/she is a little slow in getting accustomed to such habits. Moreover, buying them a new thing right after losing something, or buying them a bit too many at once for future use are not appropriate.

Helping them realize why they have lost it is most important. Your child also needs practice looking for his shoes in the shoes cabinet.

7. 정리정돈 잘하기

정리정돈을 잘하면 자기 물건을 관리하기도 쉽습니다. 또한 필기 등 학습에도 도움이 됩니다. 따라서 가방 싸기나 물감· 붓· 크레파스 등 학용품, 사물함 정리부터 연습합니다. 그러기 위해서는 정리하기 쉽게 칸이 나뉜 가방과 필통을 마련하고, 사물함마다 정리품목을 써 붙여놓는 등 엄마의 배려도 필요합니다.

또한 알림장을 가상으로 적어 알림장대로 준비물을 챙기는 훈련도 좋습니다.

8. 뛰지 않기

아이들이 입학을 하고 나면 교사들은 한두 달 이상을 실내에서 아이들이 뛰지 않도록 하는데 많은 에너지를 쏟습니다. 실외 뿐 아니라 실내에서도 아이들은 뛰는 것을 좋아합니다. 복도에서 뛰다가 사고가 나는 경우도 흔합니다. 따라서 가정교육에서부터 아이가 평소에 실내에서 뛰지 않도록 지도하는 것이 필요합니다. 왼쪽으로 사뿐사뿐 걸어 다닐 수 있도록 걸음마부터 다시 지도하여야 합니다.

7. Pick-up and organizing

If your child is organized, it will be easier for him to look after his belongings by himself. Moreover, the habit can help him improve his writing and study. Therefore, the first practice begins with packing his schoolbag, paints, brushes, crayons, other school supplies, and organizing his locker. Therefore, the mother needs to make efforts to get a schoolbag and a pencil case with divided rooms inside, and to label each personal locker stating the nature of its content. Or the mother can make up a school note on a piece of paper, have him practice preparing accordingly.

8. Not running around

For the first one or two months after the admission of the children, teachers pour their energy into keeping them from running around inside the school. Children love to run around not only outside but also inside. Children often get hurt while running in a hallway. Therefore, teaching them not to run around inside the school is also considered an important part of home education. Children should be taught to walk gently on the left, which is like teaching them how to toddle all over again.

9. 화장실 사용법

아이가 예민하면 학교 화장실에서 대변을 보지 못하는 경우가 있습니다.

갑자기 달라진 환경에 스트레스를 받아 변비를 앓는 경우들도 있으니 아침마다 화장실에 가는 습관을 미리 길들여주시는 것이 좋습니다.

자녀와 함께 학교에 가서 화장실 위치를 확인하고 사용법을 설명해줍니다. 혼자 화장실을 가본 경험이 적은 아이들에게는 아주 중요한 문제입니다. 특히 쉬는 시간을 놓쳐 화장실을 못 가는 일이 없도록 주의를 주고, 용변 보는 법과 뒤처리하는 방법을 자세히 가르쳐줘야 합니다. 화장실 구조가 집과 달라 가기 싫어하는 아이들도 있는데 이런 경우에는 엄마와 함께 외출할 때 공중화장실을 이용해보면 도움이 됩니다.

집이 아닌 새로운 환경인 학교에서 긴장한 나머지 옷에 실수하는 등 배설장애로 곤란을 겪는 아이들이 있습니다. 이때 아이가 수치심이 들지 않게 배려하며, 윽박지르거나 창피를 주지 않아야 합니다. 아이를 혼낼 경우 주눅이 들어 계속 실수를 하거나 자신감이 떨어지며 친구 관계에도 어려움을 겪는 등 더 큰 문제를 가져올 수 있기 때문입니다.

또한 실수를 했을 때는 몸에 이상이 있는 것은 아닌지, 학교생활에 문제점은 없는지, 담임선생님을 많이 무서워하지는 않는지 등 다른 이유에 대해서도 고려해봅니다.

화장실이 가고 싶을 때는 수업시간 중에라도 선생님께 조용히 말하고 다녀올 수 있도록 연습시킵니다.

대변은 등교 전 집에서 해결할 수 있도록 하고 소변은 쉬는 시간에 맞추어 볼 수 있도록 하거나, 1시간 정도는 참을 수 있도록 집에서 연습을 시키면 학교생활에 더 빨리 적응할 수 있습니다. 대변은 아침에 일어나 물을 한 컵 마시고 정해진 시간에 화장실에 가는 습관을 기르게 하는 것이 중요합니다.

특히 유치원과 달리 초등학교는 수업시간이 정해져 있고, 교실과 화장실이 떨어져 있어 아이들을 더욱 당혹스럽게 하므로 미리 학교 화장실에 들러 체험해보게 하면 좋습니다.

또한 요즘에는 비데 때문에 고학년이 되어서도 대변 처리를 못하는 아이들이 있으므로 대변 처리 훈련도 빼놓아서는 안 됩니다.

6세쯤 되면 어느 정도는 처리할 수 있도록 연습을 하여야 합니다.

9. Using a bathroom

When children become sensitive, they often cannot defecate. Children go under stress when they are exposed to an changing environment; therefore, going to the bathroom every morning is a good habit to get into.

Go to the school with your child and check the location of the bathroom and teach him how to use it. It can be a critical problem for a child who has never gone to a bathroom by himself. Warn your child not to forget to go to a bathroom at the break time, and thoroughly teach him how to use the toilet and clean it up. For those children who do not like to go to the school bathroom because it is a bit different from the one at home, using a public bathroom can help solve the problem. Some children become so tense, so they often experience a bowel problem and discharge it in their pants. At that point, you need to be considerate of his feelings and try not to make him shameful about what he did. If you scold him for what he did, he will most likely feel intimidated and continue to make same mistakes; consequently, losing confidence can cause even more problem, such as not being able to getting along with friends. You also need to look into other possible reasons when he repeats the same mistake: Is he sick? Does he have any problems with the school life? Is he really afraid of his homeroom teacher? Have him practice getting out of his classroom quietly to go to the bathroom.

Have him or her defecate at home in the morning before school and have him or her urinate in a timely manner at break time. If your child has some practice tolerating it, he/she can easily fix the problem. It is important for him or her to get the habit of defecating regularly after drinking a glass of water in the morning.

Especially, unlike kindergarten, classes at an elementary school run at fixed hours, and the bathrooms are distant from a classroom. Stopping in the bathroom and trying it beforehand can save your kid from a possible embarrassment.

Some students even in their upper grades cannot clean up after defecation because they are used to using a bidet. Therefore, cleaning the bathroom is an essential training that cannot be missed out.

By the age of 6, children should have done some practice to be able to take care of this task.

10. 제대로 손 씻기

손을 제대로 씻는 것만으로도 질병 예방에 상당한 효과가 있다는 것은 잘 알려진 사실입니다. 외출이나 놀이 후 식사 전 용변을 보고 난 뒤에는 반드시 손을 씻도록 합니다.

유치원에서도 5세 어린이는 교사가 손을 씻겨주는 경우가 많지만 6세가 되면 손에 묻은 검댕이 정도는 혼자 씻을 수 있어야 하고, 7세부터는 제대로 씻기가 가능하도록 해야 합니다. 그냥 손에 물을 묻히는 게 아니라 소매를 걷고 비누칠을 하고 손가락 사이, 손톱 밑, 손등, 손목까지 깔끔히 씻은 후 헹구고 마지막으로 수도꼭지에 묻은 비눗물을 헹구고 잠그기까지 연습시킵니다.

의외로 손을 씻지 않고, 씻더라도 제대로 못 씻는 경우가 많습니다.

학교생활은 공동체 생활인만큼 개인 건강에 유의해야 한다는 사실을 잊지 말아야 합니다.

11. 책상에 앉아 있는 습관 기르기

정해진 수업 시간과 쉬는 시간에 적응하기 위해서는 적어도 30분 이상 꾸준히 책상에 앉아 있는 훈련이 필요합니다. 처음부터 너무 오랫동안 앉혀놓으면 아이가 힘들어하기 때문에 10~15분에서 시작해 조금씩 시간을 늘립니다. 공부를 하는 것도 좋지만 아이가 지루해한다면 그림 그리기나 블록 조립 등 평소에 집중에서 잘 하는 것을 하면서 일정 시간 이상 자리를 지키게 합니다.

10. Thoroughly washing hands

It is a widely known fact that just washing hands alone can effectively keep diseases away. Make sure your kid washes his or her hands before dinner, after coming home, and after using the toilet.

Kindergarten teachers help wash hands of 5 years old, but, at least, 6 year old children should be able to wash the soot off of their hands alone, and by the time they turn 7 years old, they should be able to fully wash their hands. It is not merely wetting their hands. They should have practice rolling up their sleeves, soaping their hands and thoroughly washing between their hands, under their nails, back of their hands, and even their wrists, finally, washing the soap off the faucet and turning it off.

Surprisingly, some kids do not even wash their hands. Even if they do, they are not thoroughly washed. The school life is same as the community life, so children should not forget to look after their health.

11. Fostering habits of sitting at a desk

Having your child sitting at a desk at least 30 minutes straight is the kind of training your kid needs to adjust to the fixed class hours and break time at school. If he or she sits too long at a desk from the start, he will soon get tired. So, extend the sitting time a little longer about 10 to 15 minutes at a time. Of course, studying is good, but if he gets bored in the middle of it, have him engage in interesting activities such as drawing pictures, or building blocks that he can better focus on, so he can sit at a desk for a certain period of time.

12. 준비물 · 과제물 혼자서 챙기는 습관 기르기

자기 물건을 스스로 정리하는 습관을 들여야 합니다. "이거 치워"라고 명령하기보다 "엄마랑 같이 치워볼까?"라며 책상이나 책꽂이를 정리해봅니다. 입학 준비물을 살 때는 엄마가 혼자서 다 준비하지 말고 아이와 함께 가서 사는 것이 좋습니다. 준비물을 사온 뒤 아이와 함께 물건에 이름표를 붙이면서 자기 물건에 대한 책임감을 느끼게 합니다. 준비물은 학교와 담임선생님에 따라 다를 수 있으므로 예비 소집일에 학교에서 나눠주는 안내문을 참고해 준비합니다.

또 작은 화이트보드를 벽에 붙여두고 그날의 알림장 내용을 적어 과제나 준비물을 빠뜨리지 않도록 지도합니다. 처음에는 과제물의 70%를 엄마와 함께, 30%를 아이 혼자 해보도록 지도하고, 과제를 하는 데 익숙해지면 50%를 아이 혼자서 하도록 합니다. 1학년은 앞으로 다가올 2,3,4학년을 대비하는 기간이므로 바른 학습 습관과 생활 습관을 기르는 데 힘써야 합니다.

또한 학교의 숙제는 미리 미리 하게 해 줘야 합니다. 처음 습관을 잘못들이면 나중에 고생을 하기 때문입니다. 매일 시간을 정해주고 문제를 풀면 엄마가 함께 봐주는 식으로 버릇을 들이는 게 좋습니다.

13. 컴퓨터 사용 습관

요즘은 3, 4세 때부터 컴퓨터 게임으로 인해 부모와 말다툼을 합니다. TV도 마찬가지, TV나 온라인 교육 프로그램을 잘 이용하면 학습에 도움이 될 수 있지만 장시간 붙어 있는 것은 바람직하지 않습니다.

그렇다고 해서 무조건 떼어놓으려 한다면 오히려 아이에게 반감을 살 것입니다. 따라서 아이와 함께 공부시간과 여가시간을 분리해 시간표를 짜고, 공부시간을 잘 지켰을 경우 TV 시청 및 컴퓨터 사용 시간을 늘려주는 등 상벌제도를 정확히 실시하면서 차츰 TV와 컴퓨터에서 멀어지게 합니다.

또한 요즘은 컴퓨터를 이용한 과제물이 많아졌습니다. 그러므로 무조건 못하게 하기보다는 아이에게 주제를 주어 스스로 검색하고 자료를 꾸며보게 하는 것이 좋습니다.

또 학교 홈페이지를 함께 방문해보고, 아이와 이메일을 교환하는 등 컴퓨터를 다양하게 활용하는 방법을 찾아봅니다. TV도 프로그램을 선정해 일방적인 시청을 하지 않고 대화하며 시청할 수 있도록 합니다. 그 밖에 도서관이나 영화관 등 다른 여가 활용법을 모색합니다.

12. Fostering habits of self-preparing school materials and doing homework

You child should initiate handling his belongings for himself. Rather than telling your child like, "Move it!," say," Do you want to clean it up with me?" and go ahead and straighten up the desk and the books on the bookshelf. When you buy school supplies before starting the school, it would be better to go and buy them with your child rather than doing it all by yourself. After the purchase, you can help your child feel a sense of responsibility by labeling each item with him or her.

The school supplies could be different depending on the teacher, take the school instruction hand-out with you when you go shopping.

Also, instruct your child not to miss out any homework assignment or school supplies by hanging a small white board on a wall, and writing down the important messages received from the daily school notice. The mother, at first, helps her child with about 70% of his homework, and have the kid handle the rest 30%. When the child becomes used to the homework, have him do about the 50% of it. The first year is the preparatory period for the upcoming second, third, and forth grades, so the first graders should put their best efforts in fostering adequate study and living habits.

Furthermore, you should also instruct your child to do his homework in advance. A poor habit at the start can cause hardships later on. Studying at a certain time of the day with his or her mother helping out is a sound habit to which your child should be accustomed.

13. Habits of using a computer.

Parents and their children even as young as 3 or 4 years old often argue over computer games these days, and T.V is the same. However, if you use T.V or online education programs wisely, they can certainly benefit your child with their study. However, gluing to the T.V or computer for a long time is not a sound habit.

On the other hand, keeping your child away from them for no reason can cause an adversary reaction. To help your child gradually distant himself or herself from the T.V and the computer, it is important to make a schedule and separate the study time from the free time, and implement a reward and punishment system, which will increase the T.V viewing time and the time spent on the computer as he reasonably complies with the study time.

Nowadays, lots of homework assignment using computer has been distributed. Therefore, assigning him the topics to search and having him frame the data for himself or herself is a better way of dealing with this issue than just prohibiting the computer at all times.

Moreover, try to seek ways to use a computer in more dynamic ways, such as visiting the school homepage with your child, and exchanging the e-mails with him or her. In addition, select a particular T.V program that will allow you and your child to view while talking to each either. Seek out other leisure activities, namely, a library or a movie theater.

취학 전 알아야 할 학습 내용

유치원에서 배운 수준의 한글과 숫자만 알면 1학년 공부에는 크게 지장이 없습니다. 아이에게 책을 소리 내어 읽는 습관을 들이게 하면 읽기 공부와 함께 발표력 향상에 도움이 되고, 생활 속에서 덧셈과 뺄셈을 조금씩 가르쳐주면 진도를 문제없이 따라갈 수 있습니다.

1학년 부모들은 입학하기 전 아이의 수준이 초등학교에 입학해도 잘 적응할지를 걱정하고, 주위의 아이들과 비교하면서 욕심을 내곤 합니다. 하지만, 그러한 조바심이 아이의 학습 의욕을 잃게 하는 결과를 낳기도 하니 절대 지나친 학습을 강요해서는 안 됩니다.

한글은 쓰기보다는 큰 소리로 읽는 능력을 길러주고, 수학은 생활 속에서 놀이처럼 공부하는 것이 학습에 대한 호기심을 갖는데 중요합니다.

초등학교는 보통 4교시로 운영되며, 1주일에 하루만 5교시 수업을 합니다. 입학한 3월 한 달은 '우리들은 1학년'을 배우게 되고, 4월부터 각 교과목 학습에 들어갑니다. '우리들은 1학년'은 입학 초기 학교생활과 환경에 익숙해지는 데 중점을 둔 교육이라 크게 걱정하지 않아도 됩니다.

1. 초등학교 학습, 달라진 점 세 가지

1) 달라진 교과목 : 3월 한 달 동안은 「우리들은 1학년」을 배우고 4월부터 5개의 교과목을 배웁니다. 읽기·듣기·쓰기 등 세 권의 책을 함께 가져와야 하는 국어과목처럼 함께 챙겨야 할 것들로는 어떤 것이 있는지도 꼼꼼히 확인합니다. 수학만큼은 가정에서 꾸준히 관심을 가지는 것이 좋습니다. 과정 이해이기 때문에 어렵게 느끼는데, 한 번 놓치면 따라가기 힘든 만큼 1주일에 한 번이라도 수학책과 수학 익힘 책을 점검하는 것이 좋습니다.

Learning Content Your Child Should Acquire Before Entering School

Most likely your child will not have much of problem keeping up with the first year of study with the kindergarten level of language and math acquisition. Once your child acquires a habit of reading a book out loud, it will help him improve his reading and presentation skills. With a little bit of study of addition and subtraction in every day life, your child can easily keep up with the progress of the classwork.

Many parents of the first graders worry about the academic abilities of their child and wonder if he or she can well adjust to the school life. Moreover, the parents become greedy with their child as they compare him with others. However, such anxiety exhibited by parents often cause children to lose their motivation to study, so your child should not be forced to study.

As far as learning Korean language is concerned, help him or her develop the ability to read out loud rather than only writing, and math should be taught naturally like playing a game in everyday life, so they may become more interested in studying them, which is the most important aspect of learning.

Elementary school curricula are mostly comprised of 4 different class periods. There is a 5 class day only one day of the week. Newly admitted students only learn "We are the first graders" in March, and start the regular classes starting in April. The class, "We are the first graders," basically focuses on the adjustment to the early stage of school life and environment, so this class is not something you should worry about a great deal.

1. Three changes in elementary school study

1) Changed subjects : Throughout the entire month of March students only learn "We are the first graders" and start learning 5 different subjects starting in April. You ought to thoroughly check what books or how many books to bring to school, for example, your kid needs to bring 3 different books for the Korean language class: reading, listening, and writing books. It is better for you to consistently pay particular attention to math at home. This is a progressive comprehension subject, so many students find it difficult. If your kid missed even one class, it would be hard for him to catch up with the class, so it would be better for you to check the math textbook and math workbook at least once a week.

2) **성적평가** : 아이들에 대한 평가는 예전과 달리 시험 대신 교과활동중 수행평가로 이뤄집니다. 예를 들어 '때와 장소에 따라 상대방에게 알맞은 인사말을 알고 실천 하는가', '글을 읽고 관련 경험을 이야기할 수 있는가'. '놀이의 규칙을 이해하며 적극적이고 즐겁게 놀이에 참여하는가' 등으로 교과활동을 평가합니다. 방법은 수·우·미·양·가 대신 활동참여도나 악기 연주능력, 말하기, 듣기 능력 등을 수시로 상·중·하로 평가하거나 문장으로 기술합니다. 문제집만 열심히 풀기보다는 평소 수업시간에 열심히 활동하고 학교에서 시행하는 각종 대회나 행사에 적극적으로 참여해야 좋은 평가를 받을 수 있다는 뜻입니다.

3) **주간 학습 안내서** : 매 주말 가정으로 나가는 주간 학습 안내서에는 다음주 학습활동 안내와 함께 행사 안내나 기타 전달 사항이 적혀 있으므로 아이 방 한쪽에 붙여 놓는 자리를 마련해 수시로 확인합니다. 주간 학습 안내와 알림장을 참고해 아이가 스스로 준비물을 챙기도록 한 후 부모가 빠진 건 없는지 점검해줍니다.
1학년 수업엔 가족사진이 필요한 경우가 많으므로 여러 장을 미리 준비해 놓으면 편합니다. 종이 상자나 페트병, 안 쓰는 레고 블록 등 폐품도 잘 챙겨놓으면 유용합니다.

2. 선행학습 집착은 금물

우선 아이가 일정 시간 동안 집중하게 하는 훈련이 필요합니다. 초등학교에 입학하면 좋든 싫든 40분의 수업시간을 선생님과 보내야 하는데, 유치원에서 놀이중심의 교육에 익숙하던 아이들은 수업 시간과 쉬는 시간의 개념을 혼동하기 쉽습니다. 따라서 자신의 의견이나 생각을 전달하고 발표, 대화의 요령을 차분히 알려줄 필요가 있습니다.
간혹 아이가 한글을 떼지 못하거나 또래에 비해 학습 능력이 부족하다고 느낄 경우 막연한 불안감에 선행학습에 과도하게 매달리기도 합니다. 하지만 선행학습은 상호 의사소통이 가능하고 학습 진도를 따라갈 정도면 충분합니다.
국어는 맞춤법보다는 아이가 듣고 읽는 것을 얼마나 능숙하게 소화하는지를 점검합니다. 알림장을 제대로 쓰기 위해 엄마가 부르는 말을 받아 적게 하는 연습도 한 방법입니다.
수학은 1부터 10까지 숫자 개념을 정확히 익힌 다음, '아빠와 엄마의 나이', '저기까지 몇 발짝이 될까?' 등 생활속에서 자연스럽게 수, 거리, 공간개념 등에 친숙해지도록 하는 것이 좋습니다.
예·체능은 1학년 과정에서 간단한 만들기 관련 내용들이 많아 종이접기, 가위질하기 등 손 조작력을 키워주는 연습을 해보도록 합니다. 또 아이가 다닐 학교 운동장의 체육시설을 이용해 보면 학교생활에 대한 친밀도를 높이는 데 효과적입니다.

2) **Grading** : Unlike in the past, the class grading is based on a performance assessment rather than a conventional written test only. For instance, 'practicing appropriate greetings to a person at a certain time and place,' Can they relate to what they read?' 'Do they understand the rules of a game and actively and gladly participate in it?" Rather than giving grades like "Soo, Woo, Me, Yang, Ga," "Sang(Upper level), Joong(Intermediate level), Ha(Lower level)" or written comments will be given to their participation level, ability to playing musical instruments, speaking, and listening. In other words, the assessment will be based on the degree of their class performances, and their participation in various school events rather than just working on the workbooks.

3) **Weekly teaching plan** : The weekly teaching plan you receive every week has information on the following week's lesson plans, events and other messages, so reserve a place where it can be attached to and keep check on the plan. Check on the weekly plan and the notice so your child does not miss out on any item. It certainly is convenient to prepare many family photos beforehand because first graders often need them. If you keep some of the waste materials such as plastic bottles, and unused Lego blocks, they will come handy later on.

2. No Preview

Your child needs to have a training that will help him to stay focused on a class for a certain period of time. Once the child enters the school, he needs to spend 40 minutes of class time with his teacher whether he likes it or not. Those kids who are so used to a play-centered education at a kindergarten often do not have a clear concept on the class time and break time. Therefore, you need to calmly instruct your kid how to deliver his thoughts, give presentations, and talk.

Every now and then your child excessively studies ahead of class whenever he feels as if he has not fully mastered the basics of the Korean language yet or feels he is academically lagging behind other peers. However, the time spent on the preview should be just enough to mutually understand the class lectures and keep up with the current lessons.

As far as the language ability is concerned, you should check and see how well your kid can read and understand rather than just focusing on spelling. To make sure you kid can correctly dictate the school notice from his teacher, the dictation practice with the mother at home is encouraged. For math your child should have a clear concept on 1 to 10, and move on to 'the ages of mother and father,' and 'the number of steps from here to there' so that you child becomes more familiar with the concepts on numbers, distant, and space.

There are lots of lessons involved with using hands in the arts and physical education courses in the first year, so you need to have your child practice folding papers and using scissors. Giving your child a chance to use the exercise equipment at school, which he will be using later, can be an effective way to form his or her affinity to his or her school life.

3. 학교 수업

1) 3월은 학교생활 적응 수업 : 3월 한 달 동안은 40분 수업, 10분 휴식으로 구성된 수업을 첫째 주에는 2교시, 둘째 주에는 3교시, 셋째 주에는 4교시로 점차 한 시간씩 늘려가면서 학교생활에 적응하는 준비를 합니다. 한 달 동안 「우리들은 1학년」이라는 책 한 권으로 수업하는데, 학교생활 적응에 관한 것입니다. 학교에는 무엇이 있는지 둘러보기, 학교시설 이용법, 줄서기, 좌측통행, 사물함 정리, 친구들과 사이좋게 지내기 등의 내용으로 구성되어 있습니다. 학교에서 돌아오면 그날 배운 것을 물어보고 다시 한 번 연습해 볼 수 있도록 합니다.

2) 본격적인 수업은 4월부터 : 3월 동안 적응 수업이 끝나면 4월부터 본격적인 수업에 들어갑니다. 말하기와 듣기, 읽기, 쓰기, 수학과 수학 익힘, 슬기로운 생활, 즐거운 생활, 바른생활을 배웁니다. 한글은 쉬운 받침까지 읽을 수 있다면 수업 따라가는 데는 문제가 없습니다. 받아쓰기 연습을 시키는 것보다 글자의 획순 틀리지 않게 쓰기, 연필 바르게 잡기를 연습하는 것이 좋습니다. 수학은 숫자 10까지, 숫자에 한 자리 더하기 정도를 알고 있다면 적당합니다. 간혹 무리해서 구구단까지 외우게 하는 부모들이 있는데, 아이가 수업 수준을 시시하게 느껴 수업에 집중하지 않을 우려가 있다.

1학년은 단지 수와 친해지는 시기입니다. 구구단 1년 일찍 외운다고 수학을 잘하게 되는 것은 아닙니다. 무리하게 높은 수준까지 가르치지 않도록 합니다.

학교에서는 7월 말부터 일기쓰기를 하게 됩니다. 기뻤던 일, 화났던 일, 다음번에는 어떻게 대처해야 할지 등에 대해 말하게 함으로써 일기쓰기의 기초를 다져줍니다. 5월부터는 1주일에 한번 정도 일기를 쓰도록 지도합니다.

3. Preparing school lessons

1) The school life adaptation lessons in March : The entire set of classes in March are comprised of 40 minute classes and 10 minute break times. The length of each class gradually increases to help students adapt to new school hours: first week, 2 classes; second week, 3 classes; third week, 4 classes. For the entire month of March students use only one textbook called, "We are the first graders", which is about adapting to school life. This book is comprised of contents like checking out the school, using school facilities, standing in line, walking on the left, organizing his personal locker, and getting along with friends. Ask your child what he learned on that day at school and have him go over the lessons when he comes homes.

2) Regular classes start in April : Following the adjustment period the regular classes start in April. Students learn Korean listening, reading, writing, Math and Math workbook, Smart Living, Happy Living, and Ethical Living. Your child will have no problem keeping up with the language class as long as he or she can read simple final consonants. Language practice should be focused on making correct strokes in the right order and holding a pencil in a proper manner than simply practicing dictation. For math, knowing 1 through 10 and being able to add up to 10 are all they need to know. Some parents push their children to memorize the multiplication tables. If so, they may find the class boring and not concentrate on it.

The first year is a time to get used to numbers only. Memorizing the multiplication tables does not guarantee that your child will excel in math. Do not push your child to advance in math too far.

The students start to write their diary starting at the end of July. You simply help them lay the fundamental building blocks of writing a diary, such as, their happy and upset moments, and how they can do better next time, and so on. You can teach your child about writing a diary once a week.

4. 영어·수학보다 한글 독서 교육이 중요

입학 전 반드시 가르쳐야 할 것은 한글입니다. 요즘은 초등학교 1학년 교육과정에서 한글을 가르치는 과정이 빠져있기 때문에 한글을 배우지 못하고 올 경우 수업을 따라가기 힘듭니다. 특히 1학년 초기에 책을 잘 읽지 못하거나 받아쓰기 성적이 나쁠 경우, 아이가 자신감을 잃고 공부를 싫어하게 됩니다. 읽기·쓰기가 제대로 되지 않으면 영어, 수학 등 다른 과목도 잘하지 못합니다. 1학년 수업은 대부분 선생님의 말씀을 잘 듣고 자신의 생각을 조리 있게 말하는 방식으로 진행됩니다. 이런 수업을 잘 따라갈 수 있으려면 책을 많이 읽고 생각하는 독서 교육이 선행돼야 합니다.

5. 기초학습

아이들의 교과서를 보면 교육방향을 알 수 있습니다. 우선 교과서의 기본 학과목이 부모 세대 때와는 아주 다릅니다. 지금 시행되고 있는 제7차 교육과정은 기본 과정 이수기간을 10년으로 잡고 있습니다. 초등학교 1학년부터 배우는 내용이 반복 심화되면서 고등학교 1학년이 되면 모두 정리되는 셈입니다.

초등 저학년 교육은 아이들이 쉽게 접할 수 있는 생활환경에 대해 교육하여 아이들의 탐구심을 자극하는 내용이 많습니다. 심지어 국어와 과학, 사회, 수학 같은 분야도 생활에서 쉽게 찾을 수 있는 내용들을 다루고 있습니다.

국어는 말하기와 듣기, 읽기, 쓰기 부분으로 나뉘어져 교육되고 아이들의 적극적인 참여가 수업의 질에 영향을 미칩니다. 그러므로 초등학교 1학년이 되기 전에 독서와 일기, 듣는 훈련을 시작해야 합니다. 1학년이 되면 일주일에 몇 번씩 혹은 매일 그림일기와 독서감상문을 숙제로 써 야 합니다. 미리 연습해두지 않으면 숙제를 잘하는 습관을 만들기 어렵습니다. 그리고 일상대화를 잘 알아듣는 아이일지라도 수업시간 40분 동안 집중해서 듣기란 쉽지 않습니다. 남의 말을 귀 기울여 듣는 훈련은 수업태도에 영향을 줍니다.

1) 읽기

읽기의 경우 스스로 책을 읽는 습관과 소리 내어 읽는 습관을 길러주는 것이 중요합니다. 이런 활동은 발표력과 적극적인 성격 형성에도 도움을 줍니다.

4. The importance of weighing heavier on Korean reading than English or math.

It is the basic Korean language that your child must learn prior to entering school. There is not an available course for learning the basic Korean language for the first graders, so that it would be hard for your child to keep up with the regular classes if he has not learned the basics of the language yet. Most children end up losing their confidence and disliking study if they have a reading problem or have poor marks in dictation. The poor performances in reading and writing lead to more problems in other classes such as English and math. Most of the first year classes are run by students with good listening and logical speaking abilities. That is, reading education that requires a great deal of reading and thinking seems to be prerequisite in order to keep up with school classes.

5. Basic study

The textbooks tells a lot about the educational direction your children are heading. First of all, the textbooks deal with topics so different from the parents' generation. The 7th education curriculum which is being enforced now is actually a 10 year program. The types of education those first graders receive now are going to be repeated and deepened each year and will be all completed in the first year of high school.

The lower graders' education is mainly geared toward the living environment that most children are exposed to everyday, and it has lots of lessons that stimulate children's inquiring minds. Moreover, courses like Korean language, science, social science, and math mostly cover the content children can experience in everyday life.

The Korean language course is divided into listening, reading, and writing; furthermore, the quality of each class is heavily dependent on the active participation of the students. Therefore, prior training in reading, writing diary, and listening are needed before entering school. The first graders have to write picture diaries, and book reports either everyday or a few times a week. Such an important habit as doing homework is hard to get without prior training. Although your child is a good listener, it would be hard for him or her to actively listen to what his teacher says for 40 minutes in the class. The prior listening training definitely has an impact on his learning attitude in classes.

1) Reading

Reading out loud is considered an important habit to develop. The habit will help improve one's presentation skills and developing a positive personality.

2) 쓰기

쓰기의 경우에는 연필 잡는 법, 한글 획순도 미리 가르치는 것이 좋습니다. 요즘은 유치원생도 컴퓨터를 많이 사용하다 보니 손 글씨를 잘 쓰지 못하는 학생들이 많습니다. 연필을 제대로 잡는 초등학생이 한 반에 3~4명 정도밖에 되지 않을 정도입니다. 한글은 쓸 줄 알지만 필순을 모른 경우도 많습니다. '광'자를 쓸 때 '고'에 'ㅇ'받침을 먼저 쓰고 'ㅏ'를 쓰는 식입니다. ▢ 칸에 글씨를 바로 쓰는 연습을 많이 해 보는 것이 좋습니다. 글자를 써 보고 입학하는 아이들의 경우에는 연필 쥐는 법, 획을 긋는 순서, 글씨 쓰는 자세 등이 엉망인 경우가 많습니다. 쓰기의 경우에는 한 번 배우면 평생 가는 습관이기 때문에 올바른 지도를 받게 하는 것이 좋습니다. 한글을 바른 순서와 바른 모양으로 쓰는 연습과 재미있는 내용을 선정해 쓰도록 배웁니다. 한글을 모르고 들어가도 수업을 따라가는 데 지장은 없지만 또래에 비해 자신감이 떨어질 수 있으니 부모의 지도가 필요합니다.

수학은 아이들이 활동을 통해 개념 파악하도록 구성되어 있습니다. 수학은 수학책과 연습문제가 있는 수학 익힘 책으로 수업합니다. 교과서는 기본문제를 풀어 일정 점수 이상이 나오면 심화문제까지 풀도록 구성되어 있습니다. 엄마가 미리 교과서를 풀려보고 아이의 실력을 점검해 볼 필요가 있습니다. 단원별로 능숙하게 문제를 푸는 숙달기간이 아이마다 다르지만 진도는 규칙적으로 나가기 때문입니다. 아이가 어느 부분에서 어려움을 겪게 될지 미리 체크하고 연습하면 도움이 됩니다. 1학기에서 50까지 수를 이용해 '가르기'와 '모으기'는 아이들이 열심히 연습해야 합니다. 2학기에는 100까지의 수를 가지고 1학기와 같은 형태로 배웁니다. 1학년 때는 덧셈과 뺄셈을 빠르고 정확하게 계산할 수 있도록 훈련하는 것이 좋습니다.

슬기로운 생활은 사회와 과학 분야를 다루고 즐거운 생활은 예·체능분야입니다. 바른생활과 생활의 길잡이는 도덕교육을 다룹니다. 아이들은 이 과목들을 통해 읽고 함께 생각하고 얘기나누기를 더합니다. 그러므로 아이가 약한 부분을 보완해 주면 더욱 즐거운 수업시간이 될 것입니다.

한자공부는 모든 교과 내용과 관련이 있어 꼭 시켜야 합니다. 초등학교 교과서에 나오는 한자는 600~800자(한자인증시험 6급수준) 정도입니다. 학교 입학하기 전에 한자인증시험 6급까지는 아니더라도 7급~8급(150자) 수준의 한자를 미리 익혀두면 교과서에 나오는 낱말 뜻을 이해하는데 도움이 될 것입니다.

많은 초등학교에서 '한자 인증제'와 '줄넘기 인증제'를 실시하고 있습니다. 1학년 2학기부터 6학년 2학기까지 각자의 수준에 맞게 준비하여 통과하면 인증서를 줍니다. 모든 아이들이 인증서를 받는 것은 아니지만 평소에 연습해 두면 큰 어려움 없이 통과할 수 있습니다.

초등학교에 입학하기 전에 그림 그리기와 악보 보기, 기초체력운동을 해두면 활동 중심 수업에 잘 적응할 수 있습니다. 입학 전 아이들을 위한 겨울 교육 프로그램이 많이 실시되고 있으므로 집이나 가까운 교육기관을 이용해도 괜찮습니다. 또 태권도를 배우면 줄넘기를 포함한 기초체력운동을 같이 배울 수 있습니다.

2) Writing

It would be better to teach all the way from holding a pencil to how to properly stroke Korean words. Even kindergarteners use a computer a lot these days, so many of the first graders do not write well. Only 3 to 4 students in a class know how to hold a pencil properly. Some students know how to hold it properly, but there are many cases that they do not know the proper stroke orders. It is like stroking 'ㅗ' first and 'ㅏ' when writing '광'. They need lots of practice writing a word in ⬜. Even those students with prior training in writing before school still have lots of problems in holding a pencil, the ways to stroke, and the writing posture. In the case of writing, once they learn it, the habit of writing lasts for a lifetime; therefore, it would be better for them to learn it properly at first. The teaching of writing should be centered on instructing the proper order of the strokes and shapes of words and selecting interesting writing practices. Your child would not have a great deal of difficulties in keeping up with the classes even without any prior training in Korean. However, you may have to pay great attention to your child because he or she may not be as confident as other kids of his or her age.

Math class is designed to help students to grasp concepts through activities. A math textbook and a workbook are used in the class. The textbook is designed for students to work their way up from easy to hard questions. Parents need to check on the math ability of their child by having him work on the questions in the book. Every child requires a different length of time to master each unit, but the classwork progresses all at the same pace. It would certainly help if you can identify the units with which your child has a problem, and have him or her practice them. Learning to split and gather the numbers up to 50 is the lesson your child needs to concentrate on in the first semester. The students learn a similar lesson up to 100 in the second semester. The first graders should receive training that will help them add and subtract fast and accurately.

Smart Living deals with social and science disciplines, and Happy Living is arts and physical education. Ethical Living and the Living Guide covers ethical education. In these classes students read, think, and talk. Therefore, if you strengthen his or her weaknesses, he or she will have happier classes.

Chinese study is relevant to all class subjects, so he or she must have prior training. There are about 600 to 800 chinese characters that appear in elementary school textbooks(about level 6 Chinese certification). Although it is hard to reach the level 6 Chines proficiency through prior training, acquiring at least level 7 or 8(150 characters) before school can help your child understand the meanings of words appearing in school textbooks.

Many elementary schools run 'Chinese certification' and 'Jump-roping certification' programs. The certification process starts from the second semester of the first year to the second semester of 6th grade. A certificate will be issued to the students as they prepare for the test appropriate to their level and pass it. Not all children will receive a certificate, but it is not that hard to pass the test as long as they are prepared for it. Having prior training in drawing, reading music, and basic physical exercise can help your child adjust to activity-oriented classes. There are many available winter education programs for children prior to entering school, so your child may take a few classes at an institute close to home. Jump-roping and basic physical exercise are parts of Tae-Kwon-Do training, so take advantage of it.

취학 후 알아야 할 내용

1. 학교에서의 하루 일과

초등학교 1학년은 입학 후 약 한 달간 오전 9시에 등교해 오전 11시 경에 하교합니다. 우리들은 1학년 교과서를 통해 학교생활 전반에 대해 배우기 때문에 교과서나 준비물도 많지 않습니다. 4월부터는 4교시까지 수업하고 대부분의 학교에서 급식을 시작합니다.

1) 등교하기

등교 시각은 8시 30분 전후가 일반적입니다. 수업이 오전 9시 경에 시작하기 때문에 수업 시작 전 20~30분 전에 학교에 도착해서 수업 준비를 하도록 지도해야 합니다. 아이가 학교에 너무 일찍 도착하면 선생님이 없이 아이들끼리 빈 교실을 지켜야 하기 때문에 위험하고, 또 너무 늦게 도착하면 자습 활동이나 당번 활동에 참여하지 못하므로, 반드시 정해진 시각에 학교에 도착할 수 있도록 도와주어야 합니다.

2) 아침 자습 활동

학교에 도착하면 친구들과 인사를 나누고 제자리에 앉아 조용히 아침 자습 활동을 합니다. 그림 그리기, 학습지 풀기, 동화책 읽기 등 선생님과 미리 약속했거나 그날 제시한 자습 활동을 합니다.

3) 수업과 쉬는 시간

1학년은 한 과목당 수업 시간이 40분이며, 쉬는 시간은 10분입니다. 학습 내용에 따라 전체 학습, 개인별 학습, 분단별 학습이 이루어지고, 운동장에 나가 체육 활동을 하거나 도서실, 음악실, 컴퓨터실 등 특별 교실에 학습을 하기도 합니다.

4) 간식과 점심 급식

대개 2교시가 끝나면 간식으로 우유 급식을 하고, 4교시 후에는 점심 급식을 합니다. 식당이 따로 있는 학교에서는 식당에 가서 식사를 하지만, 대부분 학교에서는 급식 실에서 음식을 가져다 교실에서 식사를 합니다.

5) 하교하기

점심 식사가 끝나면 하교할 준비를 합니다. 이때에는 숙제와 내일 가져올 학습 준비물 등을 알림장에 꼼꼼히 적어야 합니다.

What Parents Should Know After the Admission of their Child

1. Daily activities at school

Students come to school at 9:00 am and go home at around 11:00 am for a month following their entry into school. However, there are not that many books or materials during the periods because the lessons are basically centered on learning general school life. Schools start having 4 classes and providing meals for the students starting in April.

1) Going to school

Students usually arrive at school just before and after 8:30 am. You ought to instruct your child to get to school 20~30 minutes before the first class starts, which is 9:00 am. It is important to help your child to arrive at school at an designated time because it is a little dangerous for your child to come to the class too early and stays there without the teacher, or the child may miss his turn for the clean-up if he comes too late.

2) Morning review activity

When your child arrives at school, he should go ahead greet his friends and quietly sit down and start to review the classwork. He or she should start to draw pictures, work on the workbook, read a children's book, or do the work that his teacher suggested or your child promised to do.

3) Classes and break times

First graders have a 40 minute class with a 10 minute break. Depending on the content of the class, they have either a whole class, individual class, or unit class. They often engage in such classes on the school ground, in the school library, music room, and computer lab.

4) Snacks and school lunch

Students may receive milk as a snack after the 2nd class period, and the lunch after the 4th class. Students at a school with a cafeteria eat their lunch there, but most of them eat the lunch that is brought in from the lunch facility in their classroom.

5) Go home from school

They should get ready to go home after lunch. It is the time students need to accurately write down the homework assignment and materials to bring for the next day's classes.

2. 알림장

알림장은 다음 날 준비물을 학부모에게 알려 주는 전달 매체일 뿐 아니라 학부모가 가정에서 담임선생님에게 연락을 보낼 때에도 사용하는 매개체로 활용할 수 있습니다. 그래서 아이가 학교에서 돌아오면 가장 꼼꼼하게 살펴보아야 할 것이 알림장입니다. 알림장은 수업에 필요한 준비물이나 과제, 가정통신문이나 기타 전달 사항이 적혀 있습니다. 알림장만 잘 살펴도 아이가 학교에서 무엇을 공부했는지, 어떻게 생활하는지 알 수 있다고 합니다. 1학년의 경우 3월에는 선생님이 지시내용을 프린트로 내어 주지만 4월부터는 아이가 직접 쓰도록 지도합니다. 요즘은 알림장 내용을 학급 홈페이지에 올려서 아이들이 전달 사항을 빠뜨리는 부분이 없도록 배려하기도 합니다. 따라서 학급 홈페이지를 살펴보거나 같은 반 엄마들 끼리 정보를 공유하면서 아이가 알림장을 제대로 쓰고 있는지 확인해 보아야 합니다. 알림장에 적힌 과제나 준비물, 전달사항은 꼼꼼하게 처리해서 아이가 학교생활을 성실하게 할 수 있도록 도와주는 것은 기본입니다. 학부모는 담임선생님께 조언을 구하거나 알려야 사항이 있을 때, 몸이 아파 병원예약으로 조퇴를 부탁할 경우, 특별한 사정으로 과제를 못했을 경우, 집안에 경조사가 있거나, 현장체험으로 결석을 하게 되거나 할 경우에 사용합니다.

2. Notice

The notice is a means of communicating with school parents, stating not just what to bring next day, but also a means of sending messages to the parents from a teacher. Therefore, the first thing that needs to be done as soon as your child comes home is thoroughly checking the notice. The notice includes the needed supplies for classes, assignments, a school newsletter, or other important written messages. Carefully reading on the notice will tell the parents what their child studied, and how he behaved at school on that day. The homeroom teacher prints out the notice and sends it out to the school parents of the first graders in March, but the students are instructed to write down the notice for themselves starting in April. Nowadays, the notice is often uploaded to a class homepage to ensure no one misses out anything. You need to check on your child that he has been writing down the notice accurately by checking the class homepage and sharing information with other parents in the same class. Some of the basic services we can offer to our kids is checking and preparing everything in detail from school supplies to teachers' messages in order help our children carry out their school lives sincerely. The notice can be used the other way around: when parents are seeking advice and an early dismissal from the school due to an illness, when notifying the teacher of family events, an absence because of a tour; and the child not doing an assignment because of an special situation the child was in.

3. 가정환경 조사서 작성법

입학하면 담임선생님이 가장 먼저 나누어 주는 것이 가정환경 조사서입니다.

가정환경 조사서는 학교에 따라 양식이 조금씩 다르지만, 가정환경 조사서를 작성할 때는 사실대로 작성해야 합니다. 담임선생님이 아동을 정확히 이해해야 학교생활 중에 발생할 수 있는 여러 가지 문제를 적극적으로 해결할 수 있기 때문입니다.

가정환경 조사서

20**학년도 OO초등학교 ( )학년 ( )반 ( )번

전 학년도 학반	( )초등학교 제( )학년 ( )반 ( )번 담임( )

| ① 성 명 | 한글 | | ② 전화번호 | | ③ 주민등록번호 | | – |
| | 한자 | | 집: | | | | |

| ④ 주소 | 시 구 동 통 반 번지(아파트 동 호) |

⑤ 가족상황	관 계	부	모	본교 동거 학생
	성 명			( )학년 ( )반 이름 :
	나 이	만( )세	만( )세	( )학년 ( )반 이름 :
	휴대폰			( )학년 ( )반 이름 :
	직 업		가족사항 중 특이할 만한 내용

⑥ 학생 본인의 장래희망		⑦ 부모가 바라는 장래희망	

⑧ 어린이의 특기		취미	현재 신체 이상 및 질병

⑨ 가정환경	이메일주소		도서보유현황	학습조력자	보훈대상자	유·무
			권		생활보호대상자	유·무
	소유한 자격증		⑩ 컴퓨터관련	컴퓨터보유	인터넷통신	프린터
				유·무	가능·불능	유·무

⑪ 교내특기적성 수강부서		⑫ 교과 선호도	자신 있는 교과: 자신 없는 교과:

⑬ 학원수강(전부)	

⑭ 어린이의 특징이나 담임선생님께 부탁하고 싶은 내용 (학습, 건강, 성격, 진로 지도 등)	

3. Reporting method on family background

The first hand-out you receive when you enter school is a form for the Family Background Report. Although the form is slightly different depending on the school, you need to fill it out truthfully. The homeroom teacher needs to accurately understand the family backgrounds of his students, so he can fully deal with the issues associated with his students.

Family background Report

20** year, OO Elementary School   ( )Grade ( )Class ( )Number

Previous Grade and Class ( )Elementary School ( )Grade ( )Class ( )Number, Homeroom teacher( )

| ① Name | In Korean | | ②Phone Nu. | | ③ Resident Registration Number | | | | | | — |
| | In Chinese | | Home: | | | | | | | | |

④Address   City   Goo   Dong   Tong   Ban   Bungee(Apt.   Dong   Ho)

⑤ Family Background	Relation	Father	Mother	Our school students living with you		
	Name			( )Grade ( )class, Name :		
	Age	( )years old	( )years old	( )Grade ( )class, Name :		
	Cell Phone			( )Grade ( )class, Name :		
	Job			Special things about your family		

| ⑥ Your future dream | | ⑦ What your parents want you to be | |
| ⑧This child's specialty | Hobbies | Any illnesses or diseases | |

⑨ Family environment	E-mail address		Number of books you have	Study helper	Person of national merit	Y·N
			( )books		Recipient of livelihood program	Y·N
	Certificates, licenses		⑩ Computer related	Do you have a computer	Internet	Printer
				Y·N	Possible· Not possible	Y·N

⑪Registered school class for your aptitude		⑫ Preferred subject	Confident subject: Not confident subject:
⑬Enrolled Private institutes(all)			
⑭Characteristics of the child or anything you would like to say to your homeroom teacher (study, health, personality, course of study)			

4. 결석, 지각, 조퇴

아동이 결석이나 지각, 조퇴를 해야 할 경우에는 미리 담임선생님에게 알려야 합니다. 갑작스런 일로 결석을 하게 되어 미리 알릴 수 없는 경우에는 담임선생님께 알리고, 부득이한 경우 다음날이라도 반드시 사유를 밝혀야 합니다.

결석계는 특별한 양식이 없으며 언제, 어떤 이유로 결석을 했는지 써서 보내는 것이므로 편지의 형식을 취하거나 알림장에 적어 보내도 됩니다.

결석으로 처리하지 않는 경우

천재지변 또는 수두, 홍역 등의 법정 전염병으로 인한 불가항력의 경우, 학교장의 허락을 받아 공식 행사에 참여하거나 학교 대표로 경기 등의 행사에 참여한 경우, 집안의 경조사 참여할 경우입니다. 특히 경조사에 대한 특별 휴가는 다음과 같습니다.

구 분	대 상	일수
결 혼	· 형제, 자매, 삼촌, 외삼촌, 고모, 이모	1
회 갑	· 부모 및 부모의 직계 존속	1
	· 부모의 형제, 자매 및 그의 배우자	1
	· 형제, 자매 및 그의 배우자	1
사 망	· 부모 및 부모의 직계 존속	7
	· 부모의 형제, 자매 및 그의 배우자	3
	· 형제, 자매 및 그의 배우자	3
	· 조부모, 외조부모의 형제, 자매와 그의 배우자	3
탈 상	· 부모 및 부모의 직계 존속	2
	· 부모의 형제, 자매와 그의 배우자	1
	· 형제, 자매 및 그의 배우자	1

4. Absence, late, early leave

When a student is absent, late or takes an early leave from school, he needs to notify his teacher. If you cannot notify your homeroom teacher of the absence beforehand because of an emergency, you must explain the situation to him at least the following day. The report of absence does not have to be in a certain form, you can just write it on the notice or write it in a form of letter.

When it is not counted as an absence

Some absences are not counted as an absence in the following cases: natural disaster, legal communicable diseases such as chickenpox, meals; when attending an official event with a permission of school, or competing for school at a sports competition, and family events. The special day-offs granted for the family events are specified as follows:

Types	Target groups	Number of day off
Wedding	· brothers, sisters, uncles, uncles on your mother's side, aunts, aunts on your mother's side	1
60th birthday	· parents, and the direct ancestors of their parents	1
	· uncles and ants and their spouses	1
	· brother, sister and their spouses.	1
Death	· parents and their direct ancestors	7
	· uncles and aunts, and their spouses	3
	· brother, and sisters and their spouses	3
	· grandparents, their brothers and sisters, and their spouses	3
Finish mourning of the death	· parents and their direct ancestors	2
	· uncles and aunts, and their spouses	1
	· brother, and sisters and their spouses	1

5. 전학

전학을 시키려면 먼저 다니던 학교의 담임선생님에게 그 사실을 미리 알립니다. 그 후 학교에 두었던 아동의 개인물품을 챙기고, 학교 행정실에 문의해서 급식비나 특기 적성 교육비의 미납, 환불 사항을 처리합니다. 또 해당 은행에 가서 스쿨 뱅킹을 취소해야 합니다.

그리고 이사를 한 후에는 동사무소에 전입신고를 하고 아동의 이름과 주민등록번호, 취학할 학교명이 적힌 전입신고서 접수증을 받아야 합니다. 그 접수증을 전입할 학교 교무실에 가서 내면 전·입학 처리 담당자가 반을 정해서 가르쳐 줍니다.

전학을 시킬 때에는 전학하는 날과 전입하는 날 사이에 최대한 공백이 없도록 하는 것이 좋으며, 아동은 보통 전입하는 날에도 공부를 하므로 기본적인 교과서를 챙겨 가는 것이 좋습니다. 그 외에 여러 가지 학적 서류는 학교끼리 처리하므로 크게 신경 쓸 필요가 없습니다.

6. 재량 활동 시간

재량 활동의 내용은 학생들의 자기 주도적 학습 능력을 촉진시키기 위한 창의적 재량 활동에 역점을 두고 있습니다.

현재 초등학교에서는 일주일에 2시간 정도의 재량 활동을 하는데, 그 중 한 시간은 컴퓨터 교육이고 나머지 한 시간은 학교에서 정한 자율적인 활동을 하고 있습니다. 재량 활동내용으로는 안전 교육, 환경 교육, 통일 교육, 심성 교육, 성 교육 등의 범교과 학습과 체험 학습, 실험 관찰, 조사, 수집, 견학 등의 직접 체험 학습 등이 있습니다.

7. 특별 활동 시간

특별 활동은 학생들이 집단생활을 하는 데 필요한 민주 시민 의식과 봉사 정신을 기르고 개성과 소질을 계발하는 활동입니다. 특별활동은 자치, 적응, 계발, 봉사, 행사 활동 등 다섯 가지 영역으로 나누어져 있습니다.

새로운 환경이나 상황에 적응할 수 있는 능력을 기르기 위한 적응 활동, 개인의 특기와 소질을 이끌어가는 계발 활동, 학생들 스스로 문제점을 찾아 토론하고 결정하는 자치 활동, 각종 행사에 참여하는 행사 활동, 다른 사람과 더불어 살아가는 능력을 기르는 봉사 활동 등으로 다양해졌습니다.

1학년은 특별 활동의 영역 중 적응 활동의 비중이 가장 많습니다. 적응 활동의 내용은 기본 생활습관 형성 활동과 친교 활동, 상담 활동, 진로 활동, 정체성 확립 활동 등입니다.

5. Transfer

If you are going to have your child transfer to a different school, you have to notify his homeroom teacher first. You need to clear his school locker, and ask the adminstration office to partially reimburse the unspent lunch money, aptitude enrollment fee, and other refunds. Moreover, go to the associated bank and cancel the school banking.

After moving into a new place, you need to report the transfer to the Dong office in your neighborhood, and ask for the transfer report form from them, which includes your child's resident registration number, and the name of the new school. Please take the transfer form to the new school and submit it to the person handling the transfer affairs. Then he or she will direct you and your child to his new class. It would be better to minimize the time gap between the transferring out of the old school and transferring into the new school. Also, it would be better to take textbooks to the class because the transferred child usually studies on the first day. You do not need to worry too much about the registration related paperwork because it is usually handled between the two schools.

6. Discretion activity time

The discretionary classes focus on building a freer and more creative student academic development. Currently, the elementary students spend about 2 hours a week on the discretionary activities. One of them is computer education and the other one is the one selected by the school. The discretionary activities include research projects such as education in safety, environment, unification, character building, and sex; and work-study programs such as experiment-observation, investigation, collection, and tours.

7. Extracurricular activity time

Extracurricular activities are mainly geared toward building the awareness in democratic citizens, service, and developing individuality, and aptitude skills. The extracurricular activities are divided into five different areas: autonomy, adaptation, development, service, and events.

The adaptation activity focuses on the ability to adapt to a new environment and situation. The development activity is for cultivating the aptitudes and talents of an individual. Autonomous activities help students find their problems, discuss them, and make decisions on the course of actions to take. Event activities include participating in a variety of events. Finally, the service activities are related to developing the students' ability to live with other people.

The first graders' adaptation activities are given the heaviest weight. The adaptation activities include forming basic living habits, making friends, counselling, forming a course for life, and establishing an identity.

8. 특기 적성 교육 활동

특기 적성 교육 활동은 학교 정규 수업 시간 이후에 학생들의 소질, 적성을 조기 계발하고 창의력 신장 및 인성 교육의 성과를 높이고자 실시하는 것입니다. 지도 교사는 교내 강사와 외래 강사가 있는데 각 프로그램마다 학교장이 책임을 지고 운영하기 때문에 강사나 프로그램의 수준이 높은 편입니다.

활동부서는 영어, 수학, 컴퓨터, 현악, 단소, 태권도, 플루트, 미술, 발명, 과학, 서예, 한자 등 다양합니다.

수강료도 사설 학원에 비해 저렴하기 때문에 사교육비를 줄일 수 있습니다.

또한 요즘은 맞벌이 부부가 늘어나면서 학교에서 일찍 돌아온 아이가 학원을 전전하는 경우가 많은데, 특기 적성 교육 활동을 이용하면 훨씬 안전하고 효과적인 교육을 할 수 있습니다.

특기 적성 교육 활동은 분기별 또는 학기별로 이루어지며 활동 시간은 오후 2시에서 5시 사이입니다.

9. 현장 체험 학습

현장 체험 학습은 다른 말로 가족 동반 체험 학습이라고도 하며 학교와 수업의 울타리에서 벗어나 생생한 자연환경과 다양한 체험 활동을 경험하여 교과 학습을 돕고 가족 간의 이해 증진 및 바른 인성 함양을 목적으로 하고 있습니다.

가족 단위 체험 학습은 가족 행사, 위문 봉사 활동 등의 사회적 행사, 도자기 축제, 관광 엑스포 등의 문화 행사 등에 참여하여 현장 체험을 할 수 있습니다.

현장 체험 학습을 실시하기 위해서는 일정한 절차가 필요합니다. 먼저 학교에 비치된 체험 학습 신청서(인적 사항, 기간, 장소, 학습 계획)를 작성해 약 3일 전에 담임선생님에게 신청 합니다 국내 활동은 학교장이 승낙한 기간 동안 참여할 수 있고 외국 체험은 1주일 이내로 제한하고 있습니다.

8. The specialty and aptitude education activity

The speciality and aptitude education activities are designed to develop the talents and aptitudes of the students and enhance their creativity and characters following the regular classes. There are two different types of teachers in charge, teachers from the school and outside of the school. The school principal is in direct charge of each program, so each program provides a high standard of teaching to the students.

The activity departments are comprised of diverse disciplines, namely, English, math, computer, string music, bamboo flute, Tae-Kwon-Do, flute, art, invention, science, caligraphy, and chinese character.

The enrollment fees are lower than private institutes, so the parents can save on the private education expenses. The number of two paycheck couples has been increasing recently, so many children getting out of the school start spending lots of time at private institutes these days. The students involved in the speciality and aptitude education activities receive much more effective and safer education.

The speciality and aptitude education activities take place every semester or quarterly between 2:00 pm and 5:00 pm.

9. Field trip

The field trip accompanies the families of the students in Korea. This is an perfect opportunity for the students to step out of the school boundary and into nature where the real world lies. Thus, the field trip can help the students with their studies, gaining hand-on experiences, understanding the family, and building their character.

The family field trip refers to social activities that include family events, visiting needy people to give them encouragement, and such cultural events as the pottery festival, and the tourism EXPO. There is a certain procedure that needs to be done in order to take field trips. The field trip application stored in the school needs to be filled out(personal information, period, place, and the study plan) and submitted to the homeroom teacher. The domestic field trip can be taken as long as the school principal allows it, and the overseas field trip is limited to a week.

현장 체험 학습 신청서

소 속	OO 초등학교 제 1 학년 1 반 25번
학생성명	이 하 늘
주 소	OO시 OO동 112번지 OO아파트 OO동 OO호
연락전화	OOO - OOOO - OOOO
위 학생은 본인의 자녀로서 전인적 인격향상을 위한 가족체험학습을 실시하고자 다음과 같이 신청하오니 허락하여 주시기 바랍니다.	
1. 체험 학습 과제	중국 상하이의 역사와 문화 탐방
2. 체험 학습 장소	중국 상하이와 항주
3. 체험 학습 기간	OOOO년 7월 1일부터 7월 5일까지(5일간)
4. 체험 학습 방법	직접 탐방 / 문화재 및 공연 관람

OOOO년 6 월 20 일
신청인 : 보호자 이 은 영 (인)
OO 초등학교장 귀하

결재	담임	교무	교감	교장

Field Trip Application

Affiliation	OO Elementary School, OO Grade, OO Class, OO student number in class
Student Name	Ha Neul Lee
Address	OO시 OO동 112번지 OO아파트 OO동 OO호
Phone Number	OOO - OOOO - OOOO

The abovementioned student is my child who would like to apply for the family field trip to the following place. We would like to request my permission for my child to go on the trip.

1. The Field Trip Assignment	Chinese history and cultural tour of Shanghai
2. The Place	Shanghai, Hangzhou in China
3. The Period	OOOOYear July 1st to July 5th(5days)
4. The study method	Direct tour / Observation of the properties and cultural performances

OOOOYear July/20th

Applicant : Legal Gardian Eun Young Lee (stamp)

OO Elementary School

Approval	Home room Teacher	Chief of School Affair	vice-principal	principal

10. 급식

급식은 학교에서 정기적으로 공급하는 식사입니다. 보통 우유 급식과 점심 급식이 있는데 우유 급식은 1교시나 2교시가 끝난 후 실시합니다. 이것은 아동들에게 균형 있는 영양식을 공급해 아동의 영양을 개선하고, 올바른 식습관 지도를 통해 사회성을 기르며 학부모의 식비 절감에 도움을 준다는 장점이 있습니다.

급식 식단은 영양사와 급식 운영 후원회에서 협의하여 매월 작성하며, 새롭게 작성된 메뉴는 급식비를 청구하는 가정통신문과 함께 아동을 통해 각 가정에 전달됩니다. 급식비는 일률적으로 정해져 있으며 대체로 각 가정에 전달됩니다.

간혹 간식을 준비시키는 학부모가 있는데, 이것은 교육적으로 역효과를 불러일으킬 수 있으므로 준비하지 않는 것이 바람직합니다.

11. 그림일기 지도법

그림일기를 매일 쓰는 것은 아이에게 귀찮고도 힘든 일입니다. 매일 똑같은 일들이 반복되는데 무엇을 써야 하고 무엇을 그려야 할지 답답할 뿐입니다. 이렇게 아이들이 일기 쓰기를 힘들어하는 것은 일기에 대한 개념을 잘못 알고 있기 때문입니다. 일기는 그날 일어난 일들을 나열하여 쓰는 것이 아니라 느낌을 적는 것입니다. 항상 하는 일이라도 느낌이나 생각이 다를 수 있기 때문에 같은 소재를 가지고 여러 가지로 다르게 쓸 수가 있습니다. 그러므로 느낌을 글로 표현하는 능력이 부족한 것도 아이들이 일기 쓰기를 어려워하는 원인이 됩니다.

일기는 우리의 생활을 되짚어 보게 함으로써 사고하는 능력이나 관찰능력, 그리고 표현능력을 길러 주는 좋은 수단입니다. 또한 느낌을 그림으로 표현하면서 창의력을 키울 수도 있습니다. 이 같은 그림일기의 좋은 점을 감안해 볼 때, 그림일기를 습관적으로 쓸 수 있는 태도를 아이에게 심어 주는 것은 아주 중요합니다. 여기에서 엄마들이 꼭 유념하셔야 할 점은 그림일기를 지도하는 데 있어서 무엇보다도 중요한 것은 아이의 흥미를 유발시켜야 한다는 것입니다. 흥미가 없는 곳에선 어떤 교육도 이루어지지 않습니다.

10. School Meals

School meals are provided to students regularly. There is milk and lunch. The milk is given to students either after first or second class period. This certainly has a number of advantages such as enhancing students' nutrients by providing them with well-balanced nourishing foods, building them sociality by teaching them proper eating-habits, and helping the parents with their grocery expenses. The menu for the school meals is decided every month by the school nutritionist and the school meal sponsor after a thorough discussion. The newly planned menu is sent out to each home with a school newsletter requesting the lunch money. The lunch is fixed and the notification will be sent to each home. Every once in a while, some families provide a snack for their child. This can backfire on the students and is not suitable for their education.

11. The methods of teaching the picture diary

Writing a diary everyday is troublesome and is hard work. The students fret about what to write or draw when their daily routines seem repetitive and fixed. The reason why students feel stressed about writing a diary is that many of them have a wrong idea about it. Writing a diary is not simply arraying what happened one after the other on that day. It is writing about their feelings. Although you tend to repeat things on a daily basis, you often have different thoughts and feelings about them, and you can write differently about the routine activities. Therefore, lacking writing skills can be a reason why they find it so hard to write.

Diaries is an excellent way of looking back on what they did and developing their ability to think, observe, and express. Moreover, they can develop a sense of creativity as they express their feelings through drawing pictures. Considering all the good things for the students, it is important to inculcate in students the habit of writing their picture diaries. It is important to note that making the students interested in writing is the most important part of teaching. No education is possible without any interest.

※ 다음은 그림일기 지도의 구체적인 방법입니다.

1) 아이가 그림일기 쓰는 것을 지겨워하면 강요하지 말고 형식을 변화시켜 흥미를 유도합니다.

엄마들이 가지고 있는 그림일기에 대한 고정관념을 버리셔야 합니다. 그러기 위해서는 시중에 나와 있는 그림일기 공책보다는 아무 줄도 쳐 있지 않은 공책을 마련하시는 것이 좋습니다. 때에 따라서는 그림을 더 크게 그리고 싶을 때도 있고, 글을 더 많이 쓰고 싶을 때도 있기 때문에 그림과 글의 구분이 정해져 있지 않은 공책이 좋습니다.

그림을 그릴 때도 크레파스만을 고집할 것이 아니라 매직펜이나 사인펜을 사용하게 한다거나 밑그림을 그리고 그 위에 여러 가지 잡지의 그림을 오려 붙이는 꼴라쥬 방식, 또는 먹물, 잉크, 물감 등 재료에 변화를 주면 아이들의 흥미를 끌 수 있습니다. 또한 글을 쓰는 형식도 일기체로만 쓰게 할 것이 아니라 동시나 편지글 등으로 형식에 제한을 두지 않습니다.

2) 느낌을 글로 표현하는 것이 처음에는 어렵습니다. 그러므로 엄마가 말로서 느낌을 정리해 주는 것이 필요합니다.

오늘 하루를 머리 속에 그려보게 하면서 "아침에 무슨 일을 했니?" "기분이 어땠는데?", "어떻게 하면 좋은 기분을 가질 수 있을까?" 등의 질문을 하면서 일기 쓸 소재를 찾아내게 합니다.

예를 들어 놀이터에서 놀았다는 얘기를 쓸 때 대부분의 아이들은 재미있게 놀았다는 느낌 외 에는 쓰지 못합니다. 이럴 경우에 엄마가 "시소에 앉았을 때 차갑지 않았니?", "왜 차가울까? 차갑지 않으려면 어떻게 하면 좋을까?" 하면서 쇠와 나무의 재질을 비교한다든가 다른 아파트의 시소와 비교하게 한다든가, 또는 시소의 색을 말해본다든가 해서 소재를 놀이터보다는 시소로 잡게 하는 것입니다. 즉 커다란 소재보다 조그마한 소재에서 풍부한 느낌을 유발시킬 수 있기 때문에 되도록 작은 것을 소재로 잡아 일기를 쓰게 하는 것이 좋고, 이렇게 함으로써 관찰력과 창의력을 길러 줄 수 있는 것입니다.

3) 일기쓰기의 목적은 맞춤법 공부가 아닙니다.

엄마가 아이의 일기 지도를 할 때 보면 손에 지우개를 들고 계십니다. 아이가 한자 한자 쓸 때마다 맞춤법을 교정하기 위해서입니다. 이것은 바람직하지 않습니다. 글을 쓰는 것은 머리 속의 느낌을 적는 것이기 때문에 느낌의 흐름이 중요합니다. 생각나는 대로 자연스럽게 써나가는데 엄마가 옆에서 자꾸 맞춤법 지적을 하면 흐름이 끊겨서 다음에 쓸 내용이 생각나지 않습니다. 어린아이들은 두 가지 것을 동시에 처리하기가 어렵습니다. 처리 용량이 어른 보다 작기 때문에 맞춤법과 글의 내용을 동시에 생각하기가 어렵습니다. 일기를 쓰는 목적은 우선 표현 능력을 기르는 것이기 때문에 맞춤법은 부차적인 것입니다. 그러므로 맞춤법 교정은 일기 쓰기에 흥미를 잃을 수도 있기 때문에 조금은 자제해 주시는 게 좋겠습니다. 학교에 일기를 제출하면 선생님이 맞춤법 교정을 너무 많이 해주셔서 일기가 온통 빨간색이 되는 경우가 있는데 이것도 아이의 상상력을 억제시키는 요인이 됩니다.

※ The following are the specific methods of teaching the picture diary.

1) If your child gets tired of writing a picture diary, do not force him to do it, rather, make him interested in it by changing the formality.

Mothers need to discard their fixed ideas about the picture diary. One of the changes is buying them a lineless picture diary notebook available in the market, rather than buying them a lined one. Every now and then, students would like to draw bigger pictures or write more than usual. Therefore, a notebook without a clear boundary between the picture and writing space is better.

Do not be persistent on using crayons only, have him use magic markers or high-lighters along with trying a collage style, which is drawing a rough sketch and sticking clipped magazine pictures on them; moreover, provide variety in the materials, namely, adding ink, chinese ink, or paints can attract their attention. In terms of writing style, it does not have to be limited to a diary writing like style only, but it can be written as a children's poem or letter.

2) Expressing their feelings in writing is very hard at first. Therefore, properly wording of their feelings and thoughts by mother is needed.

Have your child draw a picture of his coming day in his head, and have him find topics to write about by asking him questions like "What did you do this morning?" "How did you feel then?" "What do you need to do to make yourself feel better?"

After they played around in the playground, the only thing they can write about is that they had a great time at the place. At this point, mother can help him shift his thoughts from the playground to more specific things like the seesaw as she compares the materials those seesaws are made of, between steel and wood; or seesaws at different apartments; or colors of the seesaws by asking following questions like, "Wasn't it a little cold when you sat on the seesaw?" "Why was it cold?" "So, what needs to be done not to make it so cold?" More dynamic feelings can be drawn from small things or topics, so, if possible, make him choose a small topic and let him write about it. Consequently, the child will develop an ability to observe and obtain a significant degree of creativity.

3) The purpose of writing a diary is not just learning how to spell.

A mother teaching the diary to her child always hold an eraser in her hand ready to correct every misspelled word he or she writes. This is not appropriate. To write is like writing down the feelings in his or her heart, so the flow of writing is crucial. If the mother keeps pointing out the misspellings to the child in the midst of the flow of thoughts, it will break the flow and he may have trouble thinking of what to write next. It is hard for a child to handle two things at the same time.

The main purpose of writing a diary is to develop an ability to express oneself, and the spelling is secondary. The correcting the misspelling can cause children to lose their interest in writing a diary, so please go easy on the correction.

After submitting the diary to the teacher, his diary is often colored red with a correction marker. This factor might discourage the child from expanding his ability to imagine.

12. 학부모가 참여할 수 있는 단체

학부모는 학교에서 필요로 하는 여러 봉사 활동에 가능한 한 적극적으로 참여하는 것이 좋습니다. 요즘 학교는 교사와 학부모, 학생이 함께 만들어 가는 교육 공간이라는 인식이 강해, 학부모들의 학교 운영 참여와 도움을 적극적으로 수용하고 있습니다.

학부모 단체의 종류로는 학교 운영위원회 ,학부모회, 녹색어머니회, 명예교사회, 급식 도우미, 지역사회 어머니회 등이 있으며 각 학교의 사정에 따라서 약간의 차이가 있습니다.

1) 학교 운영위원회

학교 운영위원회는 학부모 위원, 교장을 포함한 교원 위원 및 지역 위원으로 구성됩니다. 학교 규모에 따라 5명~15명으로 조직하는데 학부모 위원은 학부모들의 직접 선거에 의해 선출합니다. 학교 운영위원이 되면 학교 헌장 및 학칙의 제정 또는 개정, 학교의 예산안 및 결산, 학교 교육과정 운영 등 중요한 학교 운영 업무에 참여하게 됩니다.

2) 학부모회 또는 어머니회

학교에 따라 학부모회나 어머니회 중 하나를 구성하거나 두 가지 모두를 구성하기도 합니다. 각 학급을 대표하는 임원 자격을 갖게 되며 자발적으로 희망하는 사람을 선출하는 것이 일반적입니다. 학부모회나 어머니회 임원이 되면 여러 가지 학교 교육 활동을 돕고, 학부모 연수, 자녀 교육 강좌, 바자회 등의 행사에 참여합니다.

3) 녹색어머니회

녹색 어머니 교통대 라고도 불리는 녹색어머니회는 아침 등교 시간과 하교 시간에 녹색 어머니 제복, 호각, 모자 등을 착용하고 학교 주위의 횡단보도에서 어린이들의 등 · 하교를 안전하게 지도하는 일을 합니다.

4) 명예교사회

명예 교사는 야외 학습, 현장 학습, 조별 학습 등 담임선생님 혼자 진행하기 어려운 수업일 경우 보조 교사로 활동합니다.

5) 급식 도우미

대부분의 공립 초등학교에서는 어머니들이 저학년의 급식 도우미를 맡아 합니다. 학기 초 반별로 급식 도우미가 가능한 어머니들을 모집한 후 순번을 짜서 교대로 운영합니다. 당번은 급식 시간에 맞추어 교실에 가서 선생님을 도와 배식과 남은 음식물 처리를 맡습니다. 의무적인 사항은 아니지만, 가끔 학교를 방문할 수 있는 자연스러운 기회이므로 가급적 신청하는 것이 좋습니다.

12. Organizations the school parents can join

It would be better for the school parents to actively participate in various voluntary activities. Schools these days are often strongly thought as educational realms run by teachers, school parents, and students; therefore, the participation of the school parents in running school is strongly encouraged.

There are many organization inviting the parents' participation: The School Operation Committee, School Parents' Association, Green Mother Association, Honorary Teacher's Society, School Meal Assistants, Local Society Mother's Association. The wordings and the nature of the organizations would be a little different depending on the school.

1) The School Operation Committee

The School Operation Committee is comprised of school parents, and faculty members including the principal. The committee is consisted of anywhere 5 to 15 committee members depending on the size of the school. The school parents committee members are voted by a direct election of the school parents. Once he or she is elected as the school operation committee member, he can take part in important decision makings such as making and amending the rules and regulations of the school, voting on the school budget, and running school curricula.

2) The School Parents' Association and The Mothers' Association

Either the School Parents' Association or the Mothers' Association, or the both can be established depending on the school. The school parents who wish to be the members of the association have a priority to get elected with a right to represent each class. The elected members of the either association help out the school education activities and participate in the school parents training, children education seminars, and bazaars.

3) The Green Mothers' Association

The Green Mothers' Association members usually wearing a uniform with a whistle, and a hat on are referred to as "Green mother's traffic Squad" that safely assist the school children heading from and to their school.

4) The Honorary Teacher's Society

The honorary teachers often work as teachers' aids when a homeroom teacher has a hard time running outdoor classes, a tour, or group study alone.

5) The School Meals Assistants

The school mothers usually assist serving school meals for the students in the lower grades at public elementary schools. In the beginning of each semester, the groups of the meal assistants are selected by class, and they take turns serving the school meals. The person on duty walks into the class on time and assists the teacher with serving and taking care of the meals. It is not mandatory, but it is an perfect opportunity for the mothers to visit the school naturally. Therefore, it would be better for the mothers to apply for the program.

6) 지역사회 어머니회

지역사회어머니회는 운동회, 알뜰 바자회 등의 학교 행사가 수월하게 이루어질 수 있도록 직접 혹은 간접적으로 도와주는 활동을 합니다.

13. 학부모 오리엔테이션과 학부모회의

각 학교마다 학부모를 위한 다양한 프로그램을 마련해서 학교를 안내하고 자녀 교육 방법을 알려 줍니다. 오리엔테이션 내용은 학교의 현황, 학교의 교육 계획, 주요 교육 활동, 1학년 교육 과정 등이고, 학부모의 학교 교육 활동 참여 방법, 가정학습 지도 방법 등의 기본 내용을 연수합니다.

또 입학 후 2주 정도 지나면 반별로 학부모회의를 마련합니다. 학부모회의는 담임선생님이 직접 교육철학과 학급 운영에 대해 설명하는 시간이므로 놓치지 않도록 합니다. 특히 이때에는 학부모들끼리 인사를 나누고 학급 대표를 뽑거나 급식 도우미와 청소 도우미 당번을 정하는 구체적인 활동 계획이 이루어지므로, 꼭 참석해서 참여 의사를 밝히는 것이 좋습니다.

14. 스쿨뱅킹과 홈페이지 등록

초등학교에 입학하면 스쿨뱅킹 자동 납부 신청서를 작성하여 스쿨뱅킹 신청을 하게 됩니다. 스쿨뱅킹(School Banking)이란 학교에 납부해야 하는 급식비, 특기적성 교육 활동비, 현장 학습비, 어린이 신문 대금 등 각종 납부금을 전산망(온라인)을 이용하여 납기일에 학부모(또는 아동)의 예금 계좌에서 학교 계좌로 자동 이체 처리되도록 하는 제도입니다.

또한 요즘은 각 학교마다 홈페이지를 운영하고 있기 때문에 아이의 아이디와 비밀번호 등을 미리 정해 알려 주어야 합니다. 홈페이지에 등록하면, 각종 무료 학습 사이트 접속이나 도서관 이용 등을 편리하게 할 수 있습니다.

6) The Local Society Mother's Association

The Local Society Mother's Association either directly or indirectly assists in running such school events as the school's sporting events and thrift bazaar as smoothly as possible.

13. School parents' orientation and meeting

Every school provides various programs for the school parents in order to introduce the school and to teach how to educate their children. The content of the orientation includes the school's present situation, teaching plans, main educational activities, curriculum for the first graders, ways for the school parents to take part in school educational activities, and home study teaching methods.

Moreover, every class should hold the school parents' meeting two weeks after the school start. You should not miss the school parents' meeting because it is the time for the homeroom teacher to directly explain the education philosophy of the school and the class operation to the parents. The parents should come to this meeting and express their willingness to participate in various class related activities. It is time for the school parents to greet one another, and to elect the class representative, and to select the meals and clean-up assistants.

14. School banking and the school web site registration

When your child enters an elementary school, you are required to apply for the school banking after filling out the direct debt application.

The school banking refers to paying for many different bills, namely, the school meals, special aptitude education activities, field trips, and children's newspapers by automatically withdrawing the payments from the parents' bank account to the school account.

Furthermore, every school runs its own web site these days, so you need to decide the ID and the password of your child and notify the authority beforehand. After completing the registration process, you will conveniently have access to many different study sites and the school library free of charge.

15. 방학을 효율적으로 보내는 방법

자녀들에게 방학은 1학기 동안의 긴장에서 벗어나 쉴 수 있는 여유 시간이고, 또 그동안 부족했던 점을 보충할 수 있는 좋은 기회이기도 합니다.

자녀와 함께 방학을 보낼 수 있는 시기는 실질적으로 초등학교 때뿐이라고 합니다. 그러므로 부모는 방학이 시작되기 전에 아동 스스로 방학 동안에 하고 싶은 일을 적당하게 정하게 하고, 그것을 어떻게 실천하면 좋을지 함께 상의해서 계획표를 세우는 것이 좋습니다. 계획을 세울 때는 기본적으로 아이에게 주도권을 주는 것이 좋습니다. 물론 계획표를 짜기 전에, 아이와 충분한 대화를 통해 아이가 원하는 목표를 정해야 합니다.

※ 방학 계획표 만들기

1) 방학계획표에 들어갈 내용
　① 잠자리에 드는 시간과 일어나는 시간을 표시합니다.
　② 아침 운동하는 시간을 표시합니다.
　③ 아침 식사하는 시간을 표시합니다.
　④ 주요 과목을 공부하는 시간을 표시합니다.
　⑤ 부족한 과목을 공부하는 시간을 표시합니다.
　⑥ 점심 먹는 시간을 표시합니다.
　⑦ 책을 읽거나 방학과제 하는 시간도 정합니다.
　⑧ 특기나 소질을 살릴 수 있는 시간을 표시합니다.
　⑨ 부모님의 심부름을 하는 시간도 표시합니다.
　⑩ 저녁 먹는 시간을 표시합니다.
　⑪ 텔레비전 보는 시간을 표시합니다.
　⑫ 일기 쓰는 시간을 정합니다.

2) 방학 계획표 만들 때 주의할 점
　① 꼭 지킬 수 있도록 만듭니다.
　② 지킬 수 없는 것을 계획하지 않습니다.
　③ 매일 꾸준히 할 수 있도록 계획합니다.
　④ 평소에 부족한 공부를 보충하는 계획도 넣습니다.
　⑤ 평소에 하고 싶었던 일을 할 수 있도록 계획합니다.
　⑥ 매일 꾸준히 운동하는 시간을 넣습니다.

15. Ways to have productive vacations

To your child the vacation is a great opportunity to get away from the tense first-semester period and to complement their weaknesses.

It is often said that the elementary school period is actually the only time in life you can have the vacation with your child. Thus, it would be better for the parents to have their child decide on what he wants to do in the vacation and you should both discuss the plans. It is better to have your child lead the plans. A thorough discussion should be a prerequisite prior to making the plans in order to help your child set the goal that he wants to reach.

※ Making a vacation planing chart

　1) The contents that should be included in the vacation planing chart

　　① The bedtime and wake-up time need to be checked.

　　② The morning exercise time needs to be checked.

　　③ The breakfast time needs to be checked.

　　④ The time to study for the main study subjects needs to be checked.

　　⑤ The time to study for weak subjects needs to be checked.

　　⑥ The lunch time needs to be checked.

　　⑦ The time for reading and doing vacation assignment needs to be checked.

　　⑧ The time to develop one's specialities or talents needs to be checked.

　　⑨ The time for running errand needs to be checked.

　　⑩ The dinner time needs to be checked.

　　⑪ The television viewing time needs to be checked.

　　⑫ The time for writing a diary needs to be checked.

　2) Things to watch out for when making the vacation planing chart

　　① Make feasible plans.

　　② Do not make unfeasible plans.

　　③ Make plans that you can carry out steadily on a daily basis.

　　④ Add a plan to study for the subjects that you have not spent enough time with.

　　⑤ Plan for things that you always wanted.

　　⑥ Add a daily exercise plan.

도움이 되는 정보

1. 입학 후 가장 많은 문제점과 해결법

1) 친구와 잘 어울리지 못해요

뭐니 뭐니 해도 가장 큰 고민은 바로 친구 문제입니다. 따돌림 받지는 않을까, 나쁜 친구를 사귀지는 않을까, 부모의 마음은 노심초사, 친구와 잘 어울리려면 어떤 노력이 필요할까요?

〈 해결법 〉

(1) 부모끼리 먼저 사귑니다.
1학년 아이들은 스스로 친구를 사귀기 힘들어합니다. 그러므로 하교 후 놀이터에서, 학교 행사에 참여했을 때 엄마들과 자연스럽게 얼굴을 익힙니다.

(2) 또래와의 만남을 주선합니다.
또래와의 만남이 많아도 제대로 다가가지 못하면 친구 사귀기는 어려울 수 있습니다. "고마워", "미안해", "반가워", "나 좀 빌려줄 수 있겠니?", "나누어 먹자!" 등 상황에 따라 건네기 적절한 말을 연습해봅니다.
부모가 먼저 아이의 말에 귀 기울여주고, 상대방을 소중히 하는 모습을 보여주는 것이 우선입니다.

2) 학교 가기가 싫어요

가기 싫다는 말은 잘 적응하지 못한다는 뜻입니다. 유치원과 달리 학교는 마음대로 옮기거나 그만둘 수 없습니다. 또한 문제가 발생할 때마다 옮기면 아이는 실패의 경험을 갖게 되어 더욱 낯선 환경에 적응하기 어려워집니다.

〈 해결법 〉

(1) 친숙하게 합니다.
입학 전 등교하는 길을 함께 걸어보고, 학교의 놀이터, 운동장, 교실, 화장실, 강당 등을 돌아보면서 친숙하게 만듭니다.
또 책가방, 학용품도 함께 고르고, 이름도 적고, 학교생활에 관한 동화책도 읽어 보며 새로운 생활에 대한 기대감을 심어줍니다.

(2) 긍정적인 생각이 필요합니다.
"이러면 선생님한테 혼날 거야", "친구들이 싫어할 걸", "이러다 꼴찌 하겠다" 등 학교에 대해 부정적인 생각을 심어주는 것은 금물입니다. 반면에 너무 재미있다는 환상도 좋지 않습니다. "이렇게 연습하면 학교 가서도 혼자 잘할 수 있을 거야"라며 자신감을 심어주는 것이 좋습니다.

Useful information

1. The most frequent problems we face and their solutions after entering school

1) I don't get along with friends

The biggest problem is related to friendship. Your child might be bullied or might make bad friends. That's the most concern parents have. What makes your child get along with friends?

⟨ Solutions ⟩

(1) Build the relationship between parents first.
Children in their first grade have difficulties in making friends by themselves. Therefore, parents should help them to make friends. Mothers have a chance to meet each other when they join school curriculum activities or when they take home children playing in the playground after school. Use these chances to know each other.

(2) Let children have more chances to meet their peers.
Even though children have many chances to meet their peers, they do not know how to approach them and make real friends. "Thanks", "Sorry", "Happy to meet you", "Can I borrow this?", and "Let's share(food)" are appropriate situational expressions for children to practice for use. Parents should listen to children first and show respect of them.

2) I don't like to go to school

To hate to go to school means that your child do not adjust himself/herself to school. A school is different from a preschool in the sense that you cannot move to another school or quit school freely. If your child move to school whenever a problem occurs, he/she(from now on, 'he' is substituted instead of 'she' and a child is represented as only 'he' for the convenience) might remember bad memories about school, ending up having too many problems to adjust with an unfamiliar environment.

⟨ Solutions ⟩

(1) Be familiar with a new environment.
You might walk with your child along the way to school, looking around the playground, schoolyard, bathrooms, halls. You might help your child to buy a school bag and school supplies and to write his name on those products. You might read together with your child a book that is related to school life, hoping that a child can wait for school life with expectation.

(2) A positive thinking is required.
"You will be punished if you do this", "Your friends will hate it", "You might get the last place in class": do not plant these ideas to your child. Fantasy about school like 'School is just fun' is not good either. You need to say to your child, "You could do it yourself if you practice many times following this instruction" and encourage your child to have confidence in himself.

3) 수업시간에 가만히 앉아 있지 못해요

초등학교는 40분 수업 후 10분 휴식을 갖습니다. 연습이 되어 있지 않다면 수업 시간 동안 가만히 앉아 있는 것이 아이들에게 버거울 수밖에 없습니다.

어릴 때부터 꾸준한 노력이 필요합니다.

〈 해결법 〉

(1) 방해하지 않습니다.
집중력이 부족한 아이들은 한 가지를 꾸준히 하기 어렵습니다. 때문에 한 가지 일을 시작하면 도중에 심부름을 시키거나 주위를 소란하게 만들어 방해가 되지 않게 조심하고, 끝가지 마무리 할 수 있게 격려해야 합니다.

(2) 집중력 키우는 놀이를 합니다.
'다른 그림 찾기' 등 집중력을 키워주는 놀이를 합니다. 또한 게임이나 책 읽기 등 어떤 활동을 하든지 가급적 앉아서 하는 시간을 늘리도록 합니다.

4) 자신의 의사를 잘 표현하지 못해요

1학년 때는 자신의 의견을 말하고 친구들의 의견을 듣는 수업이 많이 이루어집니다. 때문에 교사나 친구들의 의견을 잘 이해하거나, 자신의 의견을 다양하고 조리 있게 말하는 연습이 필요합니다.

또한 자신의 상황이나 감정을 표현하는 데 서툴러 울거나 화를 내면 친구 관계에서도 문제가 생길 수 있으므로 자신의 의사를 정확히 표현하는 연습은 중요합니다.

〈 해결법 〉

(1) 발표 연습을 합니다.
자신의 이름, 사는 곳, 전화번호, 가족관계 등 간단한 것부터 집에서 발표하는 기회를 갖게 하며, 큰 소리로 똑똑하게 말하게 합니다.

(2) 학교생활에 대해 아이와 대화합니다.
학교에서 있었던 일에 대해 대화하는 것도 좋습니다. 이때 "OO와 오늘은 무슨 놀이를 했니?", "점심시간에는 무슨 음식을 먹었니?" 등을 구체적으로 묻습니다.

(3) 책 읽기를 합니다.
다양한 책을 접하면 이야깃거리도 늘고 논리력도 향상됩니다.
책을 읽은 후 줄거리와 주제, 느낀 점, 등장인물의 행동과 생각, 그림 등에 대해서 이야기를 나눕니다.

3) I can not sit right in class

A forty minute class and a ten minute break is a regular time schedule at elementary school. Your child might have difficulties sitting right all along the class during forty minutes. It needs a lot of effort and practice to sit right from the childhood.

⟨ Solutions ⟩

(1) Don't bother.
A child who is lack of concentration can not maintain his concentration for a certain amount of time. So, once he starts a task given, don't let him bothered by errands and noises, and encouraging him to finish the task.

(2) Play games that are helpful for improving concentration.
Concentration games such as "Find out a different picture" must be helpful to play. The hours of sitting should be prolonged through reading books, games, or whatever.

4) I can not express myself

Classes frequently taken by a child in his first grade are designed to demand his effort to express himself and listen to others. So, children need an ability to understand peers and teachers and further to talk about their opinions freely but logically. To practice how to express oneself is important because poor communication might cause crying or anger while talking and produce misunderstanding between friends which blocks friendship.

⟨ Solutions ⟩

(1) Have a chance for a presentation.
A child should be given a chance to introduce himself in public and inform his friends of his name, living area, phone number and family members. When presenting, a child is encouraged to speak clearly.

(2) Talk with a child about school life.
It is good to have a talk about school life with your child. "What kind of games did you play today with 00?" and "What did you eat during lunch?" are specific questions you might ask.

(3) Read a book with a child.
IReading a variety of books gives many stories to talk about and help improve logical thinking. It is good to have time to talk about a plot, a theme, feelings, acts and thoughts of characters, and pictures after reading a book.

2. 대답하기 곤란한 질문들

엄마가 대답하기 난감한 질문일수록 아이는 더 궁금해 합니다. 왜냐하면 그 질문은 엄마 뿐 아니라 모든 사람들이 답해주기를 꺼리기 때문입니다. 이런 질문일수록 아이와 가장 가까운 엄마가 현명하게 답해줘야 아이는 호기심을 해결하고 생각을 넓혀갈 수 있습니다.

1) 꼭 제대로 답해줘야 하는 질문들에 대한 대답의 기술

아이들이 물어본 말에 무심코 답하는 것만큼 무서운 것이 없습니다. 엄마가 무심코 흘린 말 한마디가 아이의 윤리관을 형성하기 때문입니다. 아이는 부모의 인성을 물려받는 만큼 바른 인성을 가진 아이로 키우기 위해 엄마는 성의껏 제대로 답해줘야 합니다.

(1) 왜 아빠가 아니라 엄마 뱃속에서 나왔어요?

자신이 어떻게 태어났는지 잘 모르는 아이들은 대부분 생명의 근원에 관심이 많습니다. 그리고 조금씩 커갈수록 다리 밑에서 주워왔다는 식의 탄생에 대한 이야기를 듣게 되지만 정확한 과정 은 잘 모르기 때문에 엉뚱하고 재밌는 질문을 하게 되는 것입니다.

> 답) 아기가 만들어지려면 아빠 몸속에 있는 정자 세포와 엄마 몸속에 있는 난자 세포가 만 나서합쳐져야 해. 정자가 난자를 만나려면 엄마 몸속의 자궁이라는 곳에 들어가야 한 단다. 이렇게 생긴 아기는 자궁 속에서 자리를 잡고 탯줄을 통해 양분을 먹으며 무럭무 럭 자라다가 아홉 달이 지나면 세상 밖으로 나온단다. 너도 그렇게 해서 태어난 거야.

(2) 엄마는 왜 동생을 낳지 않아요?

외동아이일수록 아이들은 자라면서 '나도 동생이 있었으면 좋겠다' 는 생각을 하게 됩니다. 이 런 질문을 하는 이유는 아이들이 외로움을 느끼기 때문입니다. 부모는 아이가 친구가 부족해서 이런 질문을 한다는 사실을 인식하고 아이와 더 많이 놀아 주고 대화해야 합니다.

> 답) 동생이 없어서 심심하니? 그런데 안타깝게도 엄마가 동생을 낳기는 힘들 것 같아. 왜냐 면 엄마, 아빠 모두 일을 해야 해서 아기를 키울 수가 없거든. 또 아이를 낳으면 지금처럼 너를 잘 돌볼 수 없게 되는데, 엄마 아빠는 너에게 모든 사랑을 쏟으며 잘 키우고 싶어, 그 러니 너무 서운하게 생각하지 마. 엄마 아빠가 외롭지 않게 좀 더 열심히 놀아줄게.

2. Difficult questions to answer

The more difficult to answer to a question, the more curiosity he has on it. If the question is hard to answer for a mother, it would be for others too. And then a child is more and more curious and wants to get an answer firmly. A mother should answer to the most difficult questions because a mother is the closest person that a child has known. If a child is given an answer from his mother, he would satisfy his curiosity and broaden his view to the world.

1) Techniques to answer to the questions that require exact explanation

To answer carelessly to questions made by a child breeds bad results because a mother's answer is critical for a child to build his ethics. A child is inherited personality through attitudes shown by his parents. So, a mother should give a careful answer to questions in order to raise her child to have an upright character.

(1) Why did I come out of a mother's stomach, not from a father's?

Children do not know how to be born and they are very much curious about their origin of life. As they grow, they ask funny questions about the origin because they do not know it exactly even though they hear a story like this; 'You were picked up under the bridge'.

> An appropriate answer) A sperm made in a father's body and an egg made in a mother's body should be met to make a baby. A sperm should go inside a mother's womb to meet an egg. A fertilized egg created by the process locates itself at a right place in the womb and grows to be a baby, absorbing nourishment through the umbilical cord for nine months until he becomes big enough to be ready to get out of the womb to the world. This is the way you are born.

(2) Why haven't you given a birth to my brother?

If your child is an only child and gets older, he might wish to have his younger brother. He feels lonely as he grows and naturally asks this kind of question. Parents should recognize that he needs friends. So, you need to make an effort to be with him and to play with him more often.

> An appropriate answer) Are you lonely because you are the only child? Unfortunately, I am not able to give another birth. Your daddy is busy working and so am I. We are too busy to have another baby. If I have another child, it might not be possible for me to take care of him/her as I do for you. What I want is to raise you with care and love like the way I do now. Don't be sad. Your daddy and I are going to play with you more often and you'll not feel lonely.

(3) 아빠는 수염이 나는데 왜 전 안 나요?

하루가 다르게 쑥쑥 자라는 아이들은 점점 자신의 신체에 대해 관심을 갖게 되고 자신과 다른 사람에 대한 호기심이 많아집니다. 아이가 이런 질문을 하면 아이가 자신의 성별 특징을 이해할 수 있도록 도와주면서 남자, 여자, 어른, 아이의 차이를 정확하게 설명해줍니다.

> 답) 아빠가 수염이 나는 것은 남자 어른이기 때문이야. 아빠도 너만 했을 땐 수염이 없었지. 그런데 열세 살 정도가 되면서 몸에 근육이 생기고 수염도 나고 목소리도 굵어졌어. 청소년이 되어 남성호르몬이 흐르기 시작했거든. 남성호르몬은 남자를 남자답게 해주기 때문에 여자 몸에는 남성호르몬이 거의 없어. 그래서 여자들은 어른이 되어도 수염이 나지 않는단다.

(4) 왜 전 치마를 입으면 안 돼요?

유아기 아이들은 성별에 대한 인식이 정확하지 않아서 위와 같은 질문을 하는 것이 지극히 정상입니다. 아이가 이런 질문을 하면 정확하게 성 역할에 대한 이야기를 해주는 것이 좋습니다. 자칫 아이에게 성 역할에 대한 고정관념을 심어주지 않도록 면박을 주는 것은 피합니다.

> 답) 남자와 여자의 옷은 서로 달라. 예전에는 남자가 치마를 입기도 했는데. 언젠가부터 남자들은 바지만 입게 됐고. 여자들은 나가 일을 하면서 바지도 입게 됐어. 지금은 바지는 남자, 여자는 다 입을 수 있지만. 치마는 여자만 입는 옷이라고 생각해. 옷은 때와 장소에 맞게 잘 입어야 하기 때문에 옷을 입을 때는 내가 남자인지 여자인지 생각하면서 입어야 해.

(5) 왜 아빠랑 결혼했어요?

보통 결혼이라는 문제에 아이들은 별 관심이 없는데 어쩌다 주위에서 결혼식을 보고나면 이런 궁금증을 갖게 됩니다. 결혼은 배우자 선택, 연애 등 설명하기가 복잡하지만 아이가 올바른 결혼관과 가족관을 가질 수 있도록 아이 눈높이에 맞춰 설명해주는 것이 좋습니다.

> 답) 사람들은 어른이 되면 서로 사랑하는 사람을 알아볼 수 있어. 그런 사람을 만나면 영원히 함께 있고 싶은 마음이 생겨서, 서로 떨어져 있으면 너무 보고 싶어지고 함께 있고 싶어져. 그래서 그 사람을 위해 맛있는 밥도 해주고, 그 사람을 닮은 아이도 낳고 싶어지게 되지, 그래서 엄마는 아빠랑 결혼을 했단다.

(3) My daddy has beard but why not for me?

When a child grows fast, he becomes interested in his change of body and gets more curious about others' bodies. When a child asks this kind of question, he should be informed about the gender difference including differences between men and women as well as between adults and children.

An appropriate answer) I am an grown-up. That's why I've got beard. When I was about the same age as you're now, I had no beard. When I got 13 years old, my muscle starts to grow strong, I got beard and my voice is changed into a deep voice. When I got older and became an adolescent, male hormone starts to be produced. That hormone makes me a real man. That hormone is not produced in a woman as much as a man, so females do not have beard. You are too young to have beard yet.

(4) Why should not I wear a skirt?

It is natural to receive that kind of question from a child because a child in his early childhood has no ability to distinguish male from female. When receiving questions relative to gender, you had better explain gender roles exactly. Avoid rebuking lest a child have stereotype about gender roles.

An appropriate answer) Clothes between men and women are different. Long time ago, men used to wear skirts. However, some time ago, men started to wear pants only. Women started to wear pants when they began to work outside home. Now, it is said that pants is right to wear for both men and women, but skirts are right only for women. Clothes should be worn differently according to time and places. When you wear clothes, you should consider your gender too.

(5) Why did you marry my daddy?

Children usually do not show any interest in marriage. However, they become curious about it after watching a wedding ceremony. You can not give a simple answer about marriage as it is a complicated issue with a long-time process of date and partner decision. Therefore, you need to make yourself understood with an easy explanation when you answer to this question so that children can build a right notion of marriage and family.

An appropriate answer) As people get older, they know who to love. Once a man meets a right woman, he wants to be with her forever. He misses her so much that he wants to live with her. A woman has the same feelings as a man. She wants to cook for her loving one and produce a baby who resembles him. So, they decide to marry. That is why your daddy and I got married.

(6) 친구한테 뽀뽀해줘도 돼요?

아이들은 아직 윤리의식이 잘 잡혀 있지 않기 때문에 친구에게 좋아한다는 감정을 표현하는 것이 서툽니다. 아이가 이런 질문을 하면 부모는 어려서부터 다른 사람의 권리를 존중하고 동성이든,이성 이든 상대방을 먼저 배려해야 한다는 것을 알려줘야 합니다.

> 답) 뽀뽀는 사랑을 표현하는 하나의 방법이야. 사랑하는 사람들이나 가족끼리는 얼마든지 뽀뽀할 수 있고 외국에서는 볼과 이마에 뽀뽀하는 게 인사처럼 되어 있어. 하지만 우리나라에서는 아무한테나 뽀뽀를 하면 안 돼. 미리 반드시 허락을 받아야 해. 그렇지 않으면 상대방이 기분 나빠할 수도 있거든. 또 뽀뽀 외에도 좋아하는 마음을 표현할 방법은 많이 있단다.

(7) 아빠는 왜 거지를 안 도와주세요?

아이들은 어렸을 때부터 약자를 동정하고 도와주도록 교육받습니다. 하지만 가끔 자신이 배운 것과 현실이 다른 것을 발견하면 이를 의아해하며 이런 질문을 하게 됩니다. 이때 부모가 무정한 태도를 보이면 아이들의 마음도 차갑게 식어가므로 잘 이해시켜줘야 합니다.

> 답) 이 세상에는 자신의 힘으로 살아가기 힘든 사람들이 있어. 돌봐줄 부모가 없는 아이들이나 장애인 같은 경우가 그렇지. 그들을 돕는 방법에는 여러 가지가 있는데 구걸하는 사람들에게 돈을 주는 것도 그 중 하나야. 하지만 아빠는 구걸하는 사람에게 돈을 주기보다 자선단체 같은 곳에 기부해서 정말 필요한 사람들을 도와주는 것이 더 좋단다. 구걸하는 사람 중에는 일부러 아픈 척하는 사람들도 간혹 있거든.

(8) 왜 다른 사람의 물건을 가져오면 안 돼요?

아이들이 다른 사람의 물건을 가져오는 경우가 종종 있는데 이는 아이가 아직 소유에 대한 개념이 제대로 잡히지 않았기 때문. 부모들은 아이에게 남의 물건을 그냥 가져오는 행위가 얼마나 나쁜지 구체적으로 설명해줘야 합니다.

> 답) 모든 물건에는 다 주인이 있어. 저기 있는 장난감 버스는 네 것이고 엄마가 차고 있는 시계는 엄마 것인 것처럼. 그런데 만약 엄마가 저 버스를 말하지도 않고 동생에게 줬다고 생각해봐. 넌 네가 가지고 놀던 장난감이 없어졌으니 얼마나 속상하겠니? 마찬가지로 물건 주인이 없을 때 허락도 안 받고 가져오면 정말 속상해할 거야.

(6) Can I kiss my friend?

A child is too young to define his view of life. So, he does not know how to show his feelings of friends that he like. If you receive this kind of question, you need to let him know that he must respect other person in the first place no matter who he/she is.

An appropriate answer) Kiss is one way to show your love. Kiss is allowable anytime between loving and beloved ones as well as among family members. Kissing a person on his head and cheek is a greeting custom in some foreign countries. However, kissing anybody is not allowable in Korea. If you want to kiss somebody, you need a permission first lest you cause somebody to get angry. Another way of expressing your feelings other than kissing exist too.

(7) Why didn't you help a beggar?

Children are educated to have sympathy on the weak and help them. However, they find out that the reality is different from what they learn and ask this kind of question; why didn't you help a beggar? If you disregard the question, they will lose a chance to experience their warm heart. Use this chance to teach how to help people.

An appropriate answer) There are people who are in need like orphans or the handicapped. There are various ways to help them. You can give some money to a beggar but I prefer donation to dependable charities because they have an organized system to help people efficiently. Some beggars pretend to be sick to get more money from people.

(8) Why couldn't I take someone else's stuff?

A child might bring someone else's belongings home because he does not know the notion of ownership. You need to explain concretely that taking someone else's stuff home without telling is very bad.

An appropriate answer) Every product belongs to somebody. Toy bus over there belongs to you and a watch around my wrist belongs to me. It is supposed that I give that bus to your brother without telling you. You would be hurt if a toy you like is gone without your being informed. Likewise, if you took something home without a owner's permission, he/she would be hurt big time.

(9) 아빠는 누워서 책 읽으시는데 왜 전 안돼요?

아이들의 습관은 부모와 주변 가까운 인물들의 영향을 받습니다. 아이의 나쁜 습관은 무의식중에 부모로부터 물려받은 것. 그래서 부모로부터 배운 행동을 부모 자신이 못하게 하면 아이들은 이렇게 질문을 하게 됩니다.

> 답) 누워서 책을 보는 것은 아주 나쁜 습관이야. 누워서 책을 보면 책이 형광등 불빛을 가려서 너무 어두워지고 글자를 너무 가까이에서 보게 되기 때문이야. 그렇게 되면 눈이 나빠져서 안경을 써야 할지도 몰라.

2) 공부가 필요한 질문들에 대한 대답의 기술

아이들은 한 가지 궁금한 것에 대해 엄마가 제대로 하나만 알려주기만 해도 열 가지, 그 이상의 영역으로 관심을 확대해갑니다. 아이의 호기심에 정확하고 확실한 답으로 아이에게 사고력과 지혜를 주는 것이 좋습니다. 호기심이 많이 충족된 아이가 공부를 잘하는 아이가 됩니다.

(1) 사람은 왜 눈이 두 개밖에 없어요?

사람의 신체는 매우 오묘해서 아이들은 몸에 대해 많은 호기심을 가지고 있습니다. 아이들이 이런 질문을 하면 부모는 아이에게 인체에 대해 올바른 지식을 가지면서 자신의 몸을 더욱 사랑할 수 있도록 정확한 답변을 들려줘야 합니다.

> 답) 우리 눈이 하나일 때보다 두 개일 때 더 정확하게 잘 관찰할 수 있기 때문이야. 눈이 하나밖에 없으면 망막에서 사물을 입체적으로 받아들일 수가 없어서 제대로 보기가 어려워. 눈이 두 개가 된 것은 이처럼 망막을 통해 사물을 입체적으로 잘 보기 위해서야.

(2) 엄마, 채소 안 먹으면 안 돼요?

편식을 하는 아이에게 억지로 음식을 먹이다 보면 아이는 이런 질문을 하게 됩니다. 아이가 편식을 하면 성장에 중대한 영향을 미칠 수 있으므로 부모는 아이의 편식을 심각한 문제로 받아들이고 음식이나 조리법을 바꿔 아이가 맛있게 먹을 수 있도록 해야 합니다.

> 답) 채소에는 비타민, 무기질, 섬유질이 많이 들어 있어 우리 몸에 아주 좋거든. 비타민은 우리 몸이 활동하는 데 꼭 필요해. 몸속에 있는 찌꺼기가 밖으로 빠져나가도록 장운동을 활발하게 해줘서 변비에 안 걸리게 해주지. 그리고 섬유질은 콜레스테롤이 생기는 것을 막아준단다.

(9) My daddy is lying down on the floor, reading a book. Why shouldn't I ?

A child builds a habit as he imitates what his parents and people close do. Bad habits might be inherited by parents. If you prohibit him from doing what they learn from you, he will ask this question; Why not for me?

> An appropriate answer) Reading with your stomach on the floor is a bad habit. If you lie down on the floor, you will hid light and read a book in a bit of darkness. In the end, you will get closer and closer to your book, which might cause bad eye sight. You might end up wearing glasses.

2) Techniques to answer to questions that require professional knowledge

One exact, correct, and excellent answer leads a child to have curiosity about more than one field. You had better give an exact and clear answer to satisfy his curiosity and teach how to think deeply and wisely. A child nourished with good communication will study well.

(1) Why do we have only two eyes?

The body of human beings are so mysterious that children have lots of curiosity related to their bodies.

When children ask questions, parents get them to have right information about a human body and give correct answers to them in order to value their bodies more.

> An appropriate answer) It's because when we have two eyes rather than one eye, we can observe things more correctly. If we have only one eye, we cannot accept things three-dimensionally at the retina so that it is impossible for us to see them clearly. The reason why we have two eyes is that through the retina, we are able to see things three-dimensionally.

(2) Mon, May I not eat vegetables?

Picky-eater children ask the above question when they are forced to eat something they don't want to. Since having an unbalanced diet can have an considerable effect on children's growth, parents should take it a serious problem and change the way of cooking of food for them to enjoy eating even what they don't like to eat.

> An appropriate answer) Vegetables contain lots of vitamin, mineral, and fiber, all of which are good for our bodies. Vitamin is essential for our bodies to act. It helps activate intestinal exercise which enables the remains inside bodies to get out, resulting in avoiding constipation. In addition, fiber keeps cholesterol from generating.

(3) 왜 별은 반짝거려요?

대자연은 아이들에게 무한한 탐구의 기회를 줍니다. 대자연의 현상에서는 아이의 머리로 이해할 수 없는 것들이 많기 때문입니다. 이런 질문을 받으면 부모는 시간을 내서라도 아이에게 구체적이고 정확한 지식을 전달할 수 있도록 공부해야 합니다.

> 답) 별이 반짝거리는 건 공기가 움직이기 때문이야. 사실 하늘에는 많은 별들이 있지만 모두 반짝거리는 것은 아니란다. 지구의 대기는 바람을 타고 끊임없이 움직이는데 지구에서 멀리 떨어져 있는 별빛이 대기층을 통과할 때 별빛이 꺾여. 그 때 일순간 모였다가 흩어지는데 이때 대기 상태가 불안하면 별이 반짝거리는 거야.

(4) 이렇게 추운데 금붕어가 물속에 있어요. 춥지 않을까요?

순수한 아이들은 작은 동물을 보호하려는 마음을 가지고 있습니다. 하지만 그 정도가 겨우 본능에 머무르는 수준이므로 동물에 대한 지식을 얻고 이해하기에는 한계가 있습니다. 아이가 이런 질문을 하면 부모는 아이의 동물을 사랑하는 마음을 격려하며 제대로 된 지식을 주어야 합니다.

> 답) 물의 온도가 4℃이상이면 차가운 물과 따뜻한 물이 자리를 바꾸면서 물의 온도가 적당하게 균형을 이루게 되지. 하지만 기온이 내려가서 4℃이하가 되면 찬물이 아래로 내려가지 않고 그대로 얼음이 돼서 얼음을 보호막으로 물고기는 따뜻하게 겨울을 보낼 수 있어.

(5) 세상에는 정말로 귀신이 있어요?

경험이 부족하고 추측하는 능력이 약한 아이들은 실제 상황과 실제처럼 보이는 상황을 구분하지 못합니다. 이런 질문을 받으면 부모는 아이가 질문하는 잘 파악한 후 아이의 수준에 맞춰 합리적인 대답을 해주어야 합니다.

> 답) 세상에는 과학적으로 밝혀지지 않은 일들이 종종 일어난단다. 귀신이 있느냐, 없느냐 하는 것도 그런 문제야. 그래서 엄마도 확실히 말해줄 수는 없어. 앞으로 과학이 더욱 발전해서 이 수수께끼가 풀리길 바래. 책을 많이 읽다 보면 저절로 답을 얻게 될지도 모른단다.

(3) Why do stars twinkle?

Great nature gives limitless opportunities of exploration to children. Because there are so many things for children not to be able to understand in terms of phenomenons of great nature. When parents get this kind of question from children, they should make some free time for studying and then deliver concrete, correct information to their children.

An appropriate answer) Stars twinkle because air moves. In fact, although there are lots of stars in the sky, not all twinkle. While the atmosphere of the earth moves constantly along wind, the light of stars is refracted when the light far away from the earth goes through atmosphere. When lights gather together and soon scatter for a second, stars twinkle if the condition of atmosphere is unstable.

(4) The gold-fish are in the water although it is so cold. Don't they feel cold?

Pure children have a mind of protecting tiny animals. However since their thought lies just in the level of their instinct, they have their own limitation of obtaining and understanding knowledge related to animals. When children ask this kind of question, parents should give them correct information and encourage their loving toward animals.

An appropriate answer) When the temperature of water is over 4C, cold water and warm water exchange their places to keep balance properly. However, When the temperature is low below 4C, cold water doesn't go down and become ice. Therefore, fish can keep warm enough to live in the winter since the ice plays a role of protective wall(booth).

(5) Is there really a ghost in the world?

Children who are short of experience and guessing cannot distinguish real situation from unreal situation. When parents get this kind of question, parents should answer properly, meeting the level of children's understanding after grasping the point of the question.

An appropriate answer) Something unable to prove scientifically often occurs in the world. Whether a ghost exists or not is also that kind of question. So, Mommy cannot tell you about it exactly. I wish this mystery would be released by the development of science in the future. You could get the answer naturally while you read lots of books.

3. 전문가들이 들려주는 초등학교 1학년 학부모를 위한 지침

전문가들이 들려주는 초등학교 1학년 학부모를 위한 교육 지침입니다. 1학년 아이들은 감정이 섬세하고 아직도 사고가 미완성의 시기에 있습니다. 하얀 백지 위에 어떤 그림을 그리느냐가 사물과 인간에 대한 가치관을 형성 시켜줄 수 있습니다.

1) 다른 아이와 비교하지 마십시오

비교당하는 것은 어른이든 어린이든 유쾌하지 않습니다. 하지만 상당수 엄마들은 무의식적으로 자녀들을 형제나 친구들과 비교하곤 합니다. 이런 경험을 당하는 어린이들은 자신감과 자아 존중감도 없으며 기가 죽게 됩니다. 아이를 비교하기 시작하면 아이의 장점과 특성을 발견하기 쉽지 않으므로 절대 다른 아이와 비교하지 않는 게 좋습니다.

2) 늘 긍정적으로 표현하십시오

긍정적인 언어 사용은 사람의 미래까지도 긍정적으로 만드는 힘이 있습니다. 50점을 받아온 아이에게 "50점도 점수라고 받아왔니"라는 말보다 "그래도 50점이나 맞았니?"라는 말이 아이에게 희망을 줍니다.

3) 부모 자신이 부정적인 말을 많이 사용하지 않습니다.

부정적인 말을 꼭 해야 할 때(아이의 안전, 건강, 건전한 사고가 위협 당할 때 등)를 제외하고는 가능한 한 부정적인 말을 사용하지 마세요. 아이들은 부모들을 따라 하기 마련이니까요. 또한 부모의 부정적인 말은 아이가 부정적인 사고를 하는데 영향을 미치기도 합니다.

4) 칭찬을 아끼지 마십시오

'칭찬은 고래도 춤추게 한다'는 말처럼 칭찬은 아이에게 자신감을 심어주고 새로운 일에 도전하는 용기를 주는 마술 지팡이와 같습니다.
칭찬의 마술 지팡이도 적절히 휘둘러야 합니다. 적절한 시기란 칭찬받을 만한 행동을 보일 때 입니다. 칭찬받을 행동을 했는데 칭찬해주지 않으면, 아이는 실망과 함께 자신의 행동을 대수롭지 않게 생각 할 수 있습니다.

5) 아이에게 강압적으로 명령하지 않습니다.

"넌 지금 자야 해" 등과 같은 명령조의 말은 좋지 않습니다. 부모의 명령이나 강압은 아이의 반발심을 일으켜 부정주의를 더욱 키워 주게 됩니다.

3. Experts' tips for the parents of first grade-students of elementary school

Here are experts' tips for the parents of first grade-students of elementary school.

First grades are in the time of incompletion of their thought and sensitive in their emotion. Which picture we draw on the white paper can make children form the value of human and things.

1) Do not compare with other children.

Neither adults nor children are pleasant with being compared. However, most mothers often compare their kids with his or her friends unconsciously. Children who got those experiences have no confidence and no self-esteem, and are depressed. If we compare with others, we cannot discover their merits and characters easily. Therefore, it's better not to compare with other children.

2) Always express things in a positive way.

The use of positive language makes even people's future positive. Saying, "Did you get as many points of 50% score from the exam?" rather than saying. "Didn't you get any more than 50%? gives children hopes.

3) Parents themselves shouldn't use negative words frequently.

Do not use negative words as long as possible, except for the necessary cases of saying negative words: children's safety, health, danger of accident and so on. Children have a tendency to follow their parents' behavior. Also, parents' negative words have influence on children's way of thinking.

4) Don't spare praising.

Praise makes children build confidence and gives them courage to attempt something new like a magic stick, as the following phrase, 'Praise makes even whales dance'. The magic stick of praise should be swung around properly. Proper timing is when children take actions deserving of a reward. If we don't praise children when they deserve it, they are disappointed at it and consider their action as a trivial, invaluable thing.

5) Parents shouldn't give orders to children compulsorily.

It's not good to say in a tone of command like "You should go to bed now." The command or oppress of parents make children resist and strengthen children's negative way of thinking.

6) 자기 행동에 스스로 책임지게 하십시오.

아이가 스스로 생각하고 판단해서 결정할 수 있는 기회를 자주 만들어 주십시오. 그리고 그 결과에 대해 스스로 평가하고 책임질 수 있도록 하십시오. 이런 경험이 많은 아이들은 자신의 행동에 끝까지 책임을 지려는 자세를 갖게 되고, 말과 행동이 무척 신중해집니다.

7) 친구관계는 아주 중요합니다. 관심을 가지고 살펴보십시오.

초등학교 1학년 시기는 집이라는 울타리를 벗어나 또래집단에서 놀며 재미를 느끼는 단계입니다. 따라서 친구들과 어울려 놀고 그 속에서 재미를 느낄 수 있도록 배려해 줘야 합니다. 우리 아이들의 친구 관계가 원만한지 항상 관심을 가지고 살펴보십시오. 친구관계가 원만한 아이들은 학교생활도 능동적일 뿐 아니라 학습의욕도 높아집니다.

8) 동화 등 책을 읽어 줍니다.

어린이의 정서를 길러 주고, 마음을 풍요롭게 해 주고, 집중력을 기르는 데 동화책처럼 좋은 것은 없습니다. 특히 옛날부터 전해 내려오는 민화나 전설을 되도록 많이 들려주는 것이 바람직합니다. 지나치게 현실적이고 지식욕에 치우친 나머지 꿈이 없는 아이가 된다면 아이의 앞날을 걱정하지 않을 수 없을 것입니다.

9) 아이를 버릇없게 기르지 않습니다.

당연하다고 생각될지 모르나, 가장 지키기 힘든 요소 중 하나입니다. 예를 들어 아이는 자신이 사달라는 것을 다 사주지 못 한다는 것을 알면서도 부모에게 다 사달라고 요구한답니다. 단지 부모의 마음을 떠보는 것이지요. 따라서 아이가 요구하는 모든 것을 들어 주어선 안 되며, 그럴 필요도 없답니다.

10) 아이는 자신을 단호하게 대하는 것에 대해 두려워하지 않습니다.

오히려 아이는 우유부단하게 자신을 대하는 부모를 더 싫어할 수 있습니다. 아이는 단호한 것을 오히려 좋아한답니다. 왜냐하면 부모의 단호한 행동과 말은 아이 자신이 어떻게 행동해야 칭찬 받을 수 있는지, 혹은 부모님들이 좋아할지 배우게 됩니다.

6) Have children take the responsibility of themselves.

Make as many opportunities as possible for children to judge and decide something themselves. And then have them evaluate the result and take the responsibility of it. Children having these experiences show a certain attitude of bearing the responsibility for their actions and are very careful when they do something.

7) Friendship is very important. Watch it with attention.

The time of first grade is a phase of playing and enjoying with peers, getting out of their houses. Accordingly, we should let them hang around and feel excited when playing with their friends. Take a good look at the friendship of our children whether there is no problem with it all the time. Children who has no problem with their friendship are active at school and show strong intention of learning.

8) We should read children storybooks.

Nothing is as good as storybooks in that storybooks develop children's emotion and make their mind fruitful and enhance their concentration. It is desirable to read them especially folktales or legends as many times as possible. If children are too realistic and greedy of intellectual appetite to keep their dream, we cannot help but to worry about their future.

9) We should have children get proper courtesy.

Although it might be considered natural, it is one of the most difficult things for children to have to become habituated to. For example, children ask their parents to buy what they want, although they know their parents cannot buy whatever they ask for. Just they want to see if their parents have a mind to buy what they want. Therefore, we should not accept anything that children ask for and also don't need to.

10) Children are not afraid of being treated strictly.

Children may dislike a certain type of parents who treat them irresolutely. Children prefer being treated rather strictly. It's because parents' strict action and words make children know how they should behave in order to get loved and praised from their parents.

11) 아이 스스로 작고 보잘 것 없는 사람이라고 느끼지 않게 합니다.

부모는 "네가 뭘 알아."라고 아이를 보잘 것 없게 만들곤 합니다. 하지만 그러한 행동은 아이의 열등감만 불러일으킬 뿐 전혀 도움이 되지 않습니다. 아이를 소중하고 중요한 사람으로 느끼도록 대하여야 합니다.

12) 실수는 실수로 느끼게 해야 합니다.

가끔 부모는 실수를 죄로 만들곤 합니다. 그런 행위는 아이 자신이 자신은 '쓸모없는 아이'라고 생각하게 만들 수 있답니다. 실수는 실수로 끝내세요. 실수에 맞는 해결책과 그에 따른 대가를 알게 하면 될 뿐이랍니다.

13) "엄마, 아빠 미워!"라는 말에 당황하지 않습니다.

아이의 이런 말은 아이가 정말 싫어서 하는 말이 아니랍니다. 단지 부모가 아이에게 한 행동 또는 말이 아이 자신에게 미안해하기를 바라는 마음의 표현일 뿐입니다.

14) 아이의 책임은 아이 스스로가 지도록 하세요.

아이가 벌려 놓은 일을 대신 해주지 않아야 합니다. 사회에도 의무와 권리가 존재합니다. 아이에게 권리만 주고 의무는 대신해 주는 행동은 하지 않아야 합니다. 예를 들어 아이는 장난감을 어지럽히고 놀이 후에 부모가 대신 치워주면 안됩니다. 아이는 경험에 의해 배우게 되는데 치우는 경험을 박탈하지 말아야 한답니다.

15) 아주 작은 아픔을 호소하는 것에 너무 많이 신경 쓰지 않습니다.

아주 작은 아픔(미끄러지거나 넘어짐, 작은 찰과상)에 신경을 많이 쓰면 아이는 더욱 더 아픈 척을 하기 쉽답니다.

11) Do not make children feel like that they are not important people.

Parents tend to make children feel neglected by saying, "I don't expect that you know such a thing". However, such an action causes children to get only a sense of inferiority. We should treat children in a way that they can feel that they are cherish and important people

12) Let children recognize that they have made nothing else but a mistake when mistaking.

Sometimes parents tend to treat the mistake of children as a fault. That kind of action can make children consider themselves as invaluable children. Mistake is just mistake itself.The best way to deal with the mistake that children made is that parents should have them search for the solution of their mistake and acknowledge the result of it.

13) Be not embarrassed by the ward, "I hate Mom and Dad".

This kind of children's saying doesn't mean that they really hate their mom and dad. Children just say that kind of expression, hoping that their parents feel sorry for actions or remarks they have done to their kids.

14) Let children themselves take their own responsibilities.

Parents shouldn't take children's places in terms of their tasks when their kids cause some problems. Obligations and rights exist in any society. Parents should avoid giving children rights while taking the place of children's obligations. For example, parents have children put things away after they play with them. Parents shouldn't keep children from experiencing cleaning themselves because children can learn how to fulfill their duty by experiencing.

15) Parents shouldn't care too much about children's light pain.

It is easy for children to pretend being more sick when parents care a lot about their children's light pain such as slipping, falling down, and a little of scratch.

16) 불가능한 약속은 함부로 하지 않습니다.

우리의 아이들은 의외로 약속을 잘 기억하고 그 약속을 기대합니다. 무심결에 '성탄절에 사 줄게', '다음 주에 동물원 가자' 라는 말로 거짓 약속을 하면 안 된답니다.

약속은 필요한 것만 하고 반드시 지키도록 합니다. 그렇지 않다면 아이는 약속의 중요성도 모르게 되고 부모를 불신하게 되며 자신을 보잘것없는 것처럼 느끼며, 기분 또한 매우 우울해진답니다. 만약, 어쩔 수 없이 약속을 못 지키게 되었다면, 잘못을 인정하고 아이에게 사과하도록 합니다

17) 이해와 격려, 사랑이 가장 중요합니다.

아이에 대한 이해와 행동에 대한 격려, 사랑은 그 무엇보다도 기초적이고 가장 중요합니다.

18) 일관성 있게 아이를 대하여야 한답니다.

무엇이 되었던지 부모는 아이를 일관성 있게 대하도록 노력합니다. 일관되지 않는 것은 아이에게 혼란만을 야기 시킬 뿐이랍니다.

16) Parents shouldn't promise their kids anything especially when it is an impossible promise to keep.

Children usually remember well unexpectedly and place their hope on the promise that their parents give. Giving parents' words like 'I'll buy it to you on a Christmas day', or 'Let's go to the zoo next week' should be avoided. Only when it is necessary to promise, parents should make a promise and try to carry out their promise. Otherwise, children cannot be aware of the importance of a promise and trust their parents, which cause children to consider themselves as unimportant people and feel depressed. If parents cannot keep their promise inevitably, they should admit their fault and apologize to their kids.

17) The most important things are understanding, encouragement, and affection.

Nothing is more fundamental and important than understanding, encouragement, and affection of children.

18) You should treat your children with consistent attitude.

As parents, you should try to treat your children consistently. Your inconsistent attitude can give them confusion.

4. 우리 아이 우등생 만들기 십계명

공부도 일종의 습관이고 태도이기 때문에 어릴 때 공부 습관을 들이면 나중에 어렵지 않게 공부를 잘할 수 있다고 합니다. 아이를 우등생으로 만들기 위해서는 부모가 어떤 노력을 해야 하는지 살펴봤습니다.

1) 아이와 함께 교과서를 많이 읽어라

아이가 가장 쉽게 이해할 수 있는 낱말과 보기를 들어 교과서의 개념과 원리를 설명합니다. 아이에게 학습을 지도할 때는 늘 교과서가 우선돼야 합니다. 교과서를 정독한 뒤, 소리 내어 읽게 합니다.

2) 질문을 많이 하는 아이로 키워라

교육 잘 시키기로 유명한 유태인 부모들은 아침마다 학교 가는 아이에게 "선생님에게 질문 많이 하렴"이라고 말합니다. 질문이란 내용에 대한 이해와 생각을 바탕으로 하고 있기 때문입니다.

3) 복습보다는 예습을 중요하게 생각하라

배울 내용을 미리 공부하다 보면 자신이 모르는 것이 무엇인지 알게 되고 자신의 실력도 가늠할 수 있습니다. 모르는 부분이 있다면 보완하도록 유도합니다.

4) 오답노트는 반드시 적게 하라

오답노트를 소홀히 하는 사람치고 우등생이 드뭅니다. 틀린 문제와 이유를 기록하는 습관은 공부 방법에 대한 문제점을 찾아내는 데 도움이 됩니다. 이때 아이들 각자의 스타일을 창조해 기록하게 한다면 지루해하지 않습니다.

5) TV 시청 계획표를 만들어라

우리나라 사람들의 텔레비전 시청 시간은 하루 평균 2시간 30분. 주말이나 방학 때는 시청시간이 더 늘어나기 마련입니다. 텔레비전을 안 보게 할 수 없다면 텔레비전 시청 계획표를 짠 뒤. 그 계획표에 따라 보여줍니다.

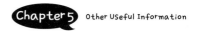

4. How to make your children top students

A learning is a habit and an attitude. So if your children have the habit for learning from their young days, they can study very well. To make your children top students, how can parents make efforts?

1) Read a textbook with your children

You can explain the idea and principle of the textbook with words and examples understandable for them. When you teach them, you should put the priority on the textbook. You make them read it carefully and read aloud.

2) Raise your children to be curious about anything with many questions

Jew parents, famous for best-educating, tell their children to ask many questions to their teachers whenever they go to school in the morning. Because the questions are based on the understanding of the contents.

3) Consider preparation more importantly rather than review

If your children study the contents to learn in advance, they can distinguish what they know and what they don't know, and judge their ability. If they have what they don't know, you should lead them to supplement it.

4) Have your children make the notebook for correction

The students indifferent to the notebook for correction cannot be top students. The habit of recording a question with wrong answers and their reasons is helpful for looking for the problems in studying. If you help your children to record them creatively, they will not be bored in doing it.

5) Make plans for watching TV

The time of watching TV of the Korean people is two hours an half a day on average. It is natural that the time of watching TV increases weekends and on vacation. If it is impossible to prevent your children from watching TV, after you make plans for watching TV, you can allow them to watch TV according to the plans.

6) 정기적으로 아이와 함께 도서관에 가라

도서관은 학교 교육이 미처 채워주지 못한 부분을 보충하는 데 더없이 좋은 공간입니다. 가족 모두 정기적으로 도서관 나들이를 해서 아이 스스로 독서 습관을 자연스럽게 들이도록 합니다.

7) 아이가 무엇을 배우는지 관심 가져라

아이가 무엇을 어떻게 배우는지 상관없이 성적에만 관심을 가질 경우 자칫 아이 인격 형성에 나쁜 영향을 미칠 수 있습니다.

8) 야단은 적게, 칭찬은 많이 하라

칭찬은 자신감 형성으로 이어집니다. 자신감이 없으면 실수가 잦아져 나중에는 의욕까지 잃어버리는 경우가 많습니다. 조금이라도 잘하는 것이 있으면 크게 칭찬하고, 실수를 했을 때는 야단치기보다 격려를 하도록 합니다.

9) 아이와 대화를 많이 하라

부모와의 대화를 통해 아이들은 논리적인 생각과 판단을 배우게 되고 그것을 표현하는 방법을 배웁니다. 정기적으로 가족간 대화 시간을 정하거나, 식사 시간을 이용해 얘기를 많이 하도록 합니다.

10) 부모가 먼저 공부하는 모습을 보여라

초등학교 아이들은 분위기에 따라 학습 효과가 크게 달라집니다. 편안하고 안정적인 집안 분위기 못지않게 늘 공부하는 분위기를 만들어주는 것이 중요합니다. 부모가 먼저 공부한다면 공부하라고 잔소리하지 않아도 아이들도 따라 합니다.

– 출처 : 초등학교 공부법(책으로 여는 미래, 조호현)에서

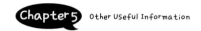

6) Take your children to the library regularly

The library is the best place to supplement the things school teachers failed to teach. Your children can have the habit of reading books through family's regular going to the library.

7) Pay attention to what your children are learning

If you pay attention to only their school record rather than what your children are learning, such your attitude might have bad influence on the establishment of their personality.

8) Praise rather than rebuke

A praise has something to do with self-confidence. A diffidence can have your children make errors frequently, and then it can make them lose a desire to do something. If your children have a spark of progress in them, you should praise them for it greatly. If they make errors, you should not rebuke but encourage them.

9) Have a lot of conversation with your children

Most of the children can learn the logical thought and judgement and the way of expressing them through the conversation with their parents. You should have the time to talk with your family regularly, or have a lot of conversation through the meal time.

10) Show your studying attitude first

The effect of learning of the elementary school students depends on the atmosphere of the house. It is important for you to make studying atmosphere all the time, as well as the peaceful and comfortable atmosphere of the house. If parents have a studying attitude rather than a nagging attitude, it is natural that the children follow them.

- the source : Guidebook for the elementary school student

5. 내 아이, 준비된 리더로 키우기 위한 10가지 전략

1) 학년별로 친한 친구 다섯 명을 사귀게 하라
아이는 스스로 생각하고 판단하는 가운데 리더의 요건을 갖춰 나갑니다. 특히 친구를 사귀는 일은 전적으로 아이의 몫이 되어야 합니다.

2) 내 아이만의 리더십 스타일을 찾아 발전시켜라
어떤 아이든 한 가지는 남보다 잘하는 것이 있기 마련입니다.
따라서 부모는 아이가 가진 장점을 발굴해 특성에 맞는 리더십 역량을 키워줘야 합니다.

3) 매 학기 열리는 반장 선거에 꼭 내보내라
실제로 경험해 보는 것만큼 좋은 교육은 없습니다.
아이는 리더의 역할을 경험하며 끈기와 이해, 도전정신, 배려심 등 다양한 능력들을 배울 수 있습니다.

4) 자존감과 성취감을 갖도록 무리한 일이나 목표를 요구하지 말라
긍정적인 자존감은 리더에게 꼭 필요한 요소입니다.
엄마는 아이가 일상의 작은 일에서부터 자존감을 갖도록 '너는 참 소중해' 등의 말을 자주 들려줘야 합니다.

5) 원활한 의사소통 능력을 키워줘라
자신의 생각을 논리적으로 표현하고 상대의 말을 경청하는 능력이야말로 21세기 리더의 가장 중요한 요건입니다.
만일 아이의 표현이 서툴다면 평소 '왜?'라는 질문을 일상화하는 것이 좋습니다.

6) 누구에게나 적극적으로 인사를 잘하게 하라
예의 바른 인사는 모든 인간관계의 시작이며 여러 사람을 이끄는 리더의 필수 요건이다. 밝은 모습으로 예의를 갖춰 인사하면 누구에게나 호감을 줄 수 있다.

5. 10 methods for top student

1) Give your children advice to make five intimate friends

You children come to prepare the top student's necessary condition through thinking and judging for themselves. In particular, you should commit making friends to your children.

2) Look for and develop my children's own leadership style

It is natural that any child has the ability to do one thing welle accordingly, parents should look for their children's merit and help them develop their suitable leadership ability.

3) Give the opportunity for running for leader election to your children

An experience is the better education than any other thing. Your children can learn various abilities such as patience, understanding, challenging attitude, and thoughtful consideration through the role of leader.

4) Don't require the excessiveness beyond your children's ability

The positive self-esteem is the necessary element for the leader. Mother should tell her children that they are very precious so that her children can have self-esteem in doing the trivial things.

5) Develop your children's harmonious/smooth communication ability

To express one's thought logically and listen to what the other man says are the most important elements for the leader. If your children are poor at self-expression, it is good to ask 'why' to them frequently.

6) Have your children greet actively

The well-mannered greetings are the beginning of human relationships and the necessary elements of a leader. The well-mannered greetings in the cheerful attitude can give a favorable impression to everybody.

7) 아이의 다양한 체험 여행을 떠나라

우물 안 개구리처럼 지낸 아이들과, 많은 것을 보고 듣고 느껴본 아이들은 사고의 폭부터 다릅니다.

세상의 다양성을 경험한 아이들은 모든 것에서 '틀림이 아닌 다름'을 인정하는 리더의 면모를 갖출 수 있습니다.

8) 대화를 통해 구체적인 비전과 꿈을 갖게 하라

리더로서의 비전과 꿈을 갖도록 엄마는 속 깊은 대화를 자주 나누며 아이의 꿈을 키워줘야 합니다. 만약 아이가 간절히 원하는 꿈이 있다면, 어떤 상황에서든 다시 일어날 수 있는 힘이 되어주기 때문입니다.

9) 다방면의 좋은 책들을 많이 읽게 하라

다양한 분야의 독서는 사고력을 향상시키고, 진정한 리더로 자라게 하는 좋은 씨앗이 됩니다. 인격이 형성되는 학령기야말로 책을 가장 많이 읽어야 할 중요한 시기입니다.

10) 부모부터 먼저 '리더'의 모습을 보여라

부모가 자신의 생각을 표현하는 데 어려움을 겪고 있다면 아이를 탓하기 전에 부모부터 리더십 교육을 받아야 합니다.

아울러 리더십 교육은 부모의 장기적이고 꾸준한 지원이 관건임을 기억합니다.

– 출처 : 예담프렌드(내 아이의 리더십. 초등 반장 선거로 결정된다)도서 중에서

7) Set out on a various trip full of experience with your children

The children who see, listen to, and feel a lot of things have the difference in the range of thought from a man of narrow view. The children experiencing the diversity of the world can have the aspect of leader recognizing difference rather than wrongness.

8) Help your children to have the concrete vision and dream through the conversation

Mother should have a deep conversation with her children and develop their dream so that they can have the vision and dream suitable for leader. If they have an earnest dream, the dream is the strength for them in any cases.

9) Make your children read multifarious good books

Reading multifarious books can improve thinking power and make your children true leaders. Your children in the stage of school age should read multifarious good books, because their personality is formed in that stage.

10) As parents, you should show the attitude as 'leader'.

If you, as parents, have a great difficulty in expressing your opinion, you should get an education for leadership rather than rebuke them. You should remember that parents' long-term and constant support is the key for an education for leadership.

- Source : Yae Dam Friend(The leadership of my child is very much affected by a presidential election of elementary school.)

6. 참고사이트와 도서

첫 아이를 학교에 보내는 엄마의 머릿속은 엉킨 실타래처럼 복잡합니다. 그래도 주위에 든든한 지원군이 많습니다. 초등학교 엄마들이 참고할 만한 사이트와 책을 모았습니다.

1) 엘레맘 (www.elemom.com)

초등학교 아이를 둔 어머니들의 모임으로 학교생활에서 일어날 수 있는 다양한 문제를 그 분야의 전문가 선생님의 도움을 받아서 상담 받을 수 있습니다. 또 각 학교 학급별로 올려놓은 시간표가 있어 아이의 학급 시간표를 확인하는 데도 도움을 줍니다.

2) 자녀 지도를 위한 부모넷 (www.bumonet.or.kr)

서울시와 서울시청소년상담지원센터에서 함께 운영하는 사이트로 정부에서 지원하는 다양한 학습 관련 기관과 상담 업무에 관한 자료를 쉽게 파악할 수 있습니다.
학부모 사이의 커뮤니티를 지원하고 있어서 온라인에서 학부모끼리 쉽게 대화할 수 있습니다.

3) 초등학교 입학 전 부모 숙제 50가지 (김정애 저, 영진미디어)

저자는 현직 교사로 10년 동안 학교에서 아이들과 생활하면서 부모 세대와 달라진 학교모습에 대해 설명하고 있습니다. 앞으로 입학하는 아이들을 위해 무엇을 준비해야 하는지 친절하게 알려주며 학교생활의 실질적인 모습을 설명하기 때문에 아이의 학교생활을 이해하는데 도움을 줍니다.

4) 첫 아이 학교 보내기 (박경진 저, 보리출판사)

현재 학교 실정에 맞게 개정되어 나온 책으로 학교를 보내기 전 준비해야 할 물품부터 입학 후 아이들이 학교에 적응할 수 있도록 도와주는 방법을 친절하게 설명해주고 있습니다. 또 부모들이 걱정하는 '촌지'와 '왕따' 이야기처럼 현실적인 이야기도 실려 있어 '아이 학교 보내기 대백과' 역할을 합니다.

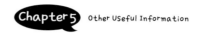

6. References (Websites and books)

A mother having her first child who just enters a school has a lot of complicated thoughts like a tangled skein. However, she has many dependable supporters around her. We listed websites and books which can be helpful to mothers as following.

1) Elemom (www.elemom.com)

This site is for mothers who have schoolchildren. You can consult a variety of problems caused in school life with professional consultants at this site. Class schedules of Schools are uploaded on this site, which will be helpful when you check a class schedule of your child.

2) Bumonet for Children guidance (www.bumonet.or.kr)

This site is run by Seoul City and Seoul juvenile consultation center. You can easily access a lot of information on consultation and learning centers supported by the government. Since this site runs a parents' community, parents can talk easily on-line.

3) 50 homework assigned to parents whose children are about to enter an elementary school (Kim, Joeng-Ae. Yoengjin Media)

The author of this book writes about current school-life that has changed a lot compared with parents' from his 10 year experience with students as a teacher. This book will guide parents how to prepare things for their children who are about to be an elementary school student and it describes the reality of school life which is helpful for parents to understand their children better.

4) Sending your first child to school (Park, Kyeong-Jin. Bori Publication)

This book was revised to reflect a current school system. More information from things you need to prepare before admission to the ways to help your child to adapt to a school after admission was added. This book also contains many real stories about bullying or a small gift (dirty cash) which parents are mostly concerned about. So, it has a nick name of 'an encyclopaedia of sending a child to school'.

5) 엄마 학교 (서형숙 저, 큰솔 출판사)

저자는 자녀 교육 전문가, 아이의 눈에 맞춰 교육하고 아이와 편안하게 대화하는 방법을 쉽게 설명했습니다. 아이가 학교에 입학하기 전 알아야 할 실질적인 내용과 어떠한 교육이 진정한 교육인가에 대한 해답을 전하는 책입니다.

6) 조커 (문학과지성사)

기발한 아이디어로 아이들에게 교과서에 결코 배울 수 없는 가르침을 주는 할아버지 선생님의 이야기입니다. 새 학기가 시작되어 기대와 두려움을 새로운 담임선생님을 기다리는 아이들, 그러나 아이들 앞에 나타난 노엘 선생님은 그들의 기대를 여지없이 무너뜨립니다. 주름투성이에다가 배가 공만 하고 흰 머리가 사방으로 뻗친 할아버지 선생님이었습니다.

7) 여우네 학교가기 (강용숙 저, 꿈소담이)

뻐기기 좋아하는 아빠 여우는 아이들을 학교에 보내 훌륭하게 키우고 싶어 동물 학교에 가는데, 원숭이 교장은 여우는 교활하다며 받아 줄 수 없다고 합니다. 교장에게 협박도 하고, 뇌물도 줘 보지만 아무런 소용이 없는데··· 마치 이솝 우화를 보는 듯한 재기 발랄한 한 편의 우화, 믿지 않은 교활한 여우를 통해 우리가 가져야 할 진정한 가치는 무엇인지 쉽고 재미있게 알려줍니다.

8) 첫 아이 학교보내기 (주순중 저, 보리)

첫 아이 학교 보내는 학부모는 아이보다 더 떨릴법합니다. 우리 아이가 학교 가서 공부는 잘 할까, 친구들과 잘 지낼까, 좋은 담임선생님을 만날 수 있을까, 현직 초등학교 교사 주순중씨가 쓴 이 책은 수년간 1학년 학생을 수백 명 접한 경험이기에 더 값집니다. 입학통지서 챙기고 소집일 출석하는 일부터 연필과 공책, 준비물 챙기기, 옷차림, 상-벌 같은 교실 현장의 구체적 내용이 들어 있습니다.

5) Mother School (Seo, Hyung-sook. Keunsol Publication)

Its author is an expert on children education. He explained in an easy way how to educate their children appropriately to their level and how to communicate with them comfortably. This book gives an useful information on admission and states clearly what a true education is.

6) Joker (Literature and Intelligence Publication)

This book is about an old teacher who teaches his students with creative methods things that they cannot learn through books. Starting a new semester, children wait for their class teacher with expectations and fears. Finally, their teacher, Noel, shows up in class. He is totally different from what they expect. He is an old teacher whose face has many wrinkles, whose belly is as big as a ball and whose white hair is stretched up at every direction.

7) A fox family, goes to school!! (Kang, Yong-sook. Kkumsodami Publication)

A father fox who is proud of himself wants to raise his children to be great through school programs. However, a monkey principal does not allow them to enter a school because he thinks a fox is cunning. It is no use threatening the principle and offering him a bribe ... Its story is kind of a funny and lively fable like Aesop's. It gives us a chance to know what is a true value that we should pursue through a story of a cunning but sweet fox.

8) Sending your first child to school (Joo, Soon-joong. Bori Publication)

It seems that parents who send their first child to school are more excited than their children. 'Can my child study well?', 'Can my child get along with his friends?' or 'Can my child meet a nice class teacher?'

The book is written by Joo, Soon-joong who is an elementary school teacher now. He has been in charge of many kinds of first grade children for years, which makes this book more valuable to read. The book includes very specific ways to deal with actual things you face at school such as packing an admission paper, pencils and notebooks before walking away from home, attending an orientation, wearing clothes and reward and punishment.

9) 아이의 인생은 초등학교에 달려 있다 (신의진, 중앙M&B)

엄마만 찾는 아이, 스스로 할 줄 모르는 아이, 공부하기 싫어하는 아이, 아이가 초등학교에 입학했을 때 흔히 보이는 증상입니다. 저자는 그 까닭으로 아이에게 요구하는 어른들의 '기대치'가 너무 높기 때문이라고 말합니다. 아이에게 초등학교는 새로운 세상이며 적응할 시간이 필요한데도 부모의 기대는 계속됩니다. 아이에게 중요한 것은 세상을 좋아하게끔 하는 일이라고 합니다. 그래야만 학업과 학교생활을 즐길 수 있기 때문입니다.

10) 학교 안 갈 거야 (토니 로스 저, 베틀북)

학교 처음 가는 아이, 이 아이는 학교에 대한 두려움이 가득합니다. 학교가 아마 무서운 괴물로 심리 속에 자리 잡았을 거예요. 엄마는 아이와 옥신각신하며 학교의 좋은 점에 대해 이야기하며 아이를 달립니다. 하지만 막상 학교를 간 아이는 새로운 친구를 사귀어 학교에 점차 적응을 합니다.

11) 우리 아이 꼭 시리즈 (중앙M&B)

'우리 아이 꼭 시리즈 ⑦초등학교 1학년' 편에서는 학교 일과, 교과서 구성, 선생님과의 관계, 알림장 관리, 체험학습 신청, 학습지 선택 등의 고민에 대해 하나하나 답을 풀어나가고 있습니다. 구체적인 사례를 통해 생활 잘하게 만드는 다섯 가지 적응 훈련법을 제시하고 있습니다.

12) 칠판 앞에 나가기 싫어 (다니엘 포세트 저, 비룡소)

목요일만 되면 선생님이 칠판 앞으로 불러 구구단을 외우게 할까봐 배가 아픈 에르만, 그러던 에르만이 어느 날 스스로 칠판 앞으로 나가 구구단을 외우는 기적이 일어나는데...발표하기를 싫어하는 아이의 심리가 아주 잘 그려져 있고 그것을 극복하는 과정이 따뜻하게 전개됩니다.

13) 선생님이 꼼꼼하게 알려주는 초등 1학년 365일 (이현진 저, 위즈덤하우스)

새내기 학부모들을 위한 입학 준비 노하우와 학교생활의 모든 것이 담겨 있습니다. 내 아이 1등 만드는 초등 1학년 완벽 가이드라고 할 수 있는 책 속에서는 현직 초등학교 교사가 구체적인 사례를 통해 꼼꼼하게 일러주고 있어, 입학 준비부터 겨울방학까지 초등 1학년을 알차게 준비할 수 있게 해줍니다.

9) An elementary school is crucial to your child's life (Shin, Euy-jin. Joongang M&B)

A child who follows only his mom. A child who cannot do anything by himself without his mom's help. A child who dislikes studying; we often see these children in their first grade. The author of this book suggests that these children receive higher expectation than they deserve from their parents. Children take time to adjust themselves to a new environment but parents expect them to do well from the right moment after admission. The important thing is for them to see the world positively. In doing so, they can enjoy their studying and school life.

10) I will not go to school (Tony Rose. Bettlebook)

A child who just enters a school is full of fear of going to school. A school might be recognized as a monster in his mind. A mother tries to convince her child to like school life with sweet talks. A child starts to be familiar with a new environment while making new friends at school.

11) For your child, 'Surely series' (Joongang M&B)

'For your child, Surely series, the 7th' gives you an answer precisely about daily life at school, contents of texts, relationships with teachers, notice check-up, application for field trip, choice of home-school materials and so on. With concrete examples, this book suggests 5 adaptation training methods that help children to have better school life.

12) I hate to stand in front of the blackboard. (Danielle Fossette. Biryongso)

Erman suffers from stomachache on every Thursday for fear that his teacher call him out to the front of the blackboard and have him memorize multiplication tables. One day, a miracle that Erman who did his routine on every Thursday successfully happened. The psychological barriers to stop a child like Erman from standing in public are described specifically and also a process of how to overcome them is in detail written, which moves a reader's heart.

13) 365 days of 1st grade at Elementary school, of which a teacher inform readers (Lee, Hyun-jin. Wisdom house)

This book includes live school-life stories and preparatory know-how parents with 1st grade children. It deserves to have a title as 'A perfect guideline for a 1st grade student to become top in class'. Its author is an elementary school teacher and his/her advice helps parents to prepare what they have to do for their children from the moment of school entrance to winter vacation, with examples provided.

14) 지각 대장 존 (존 버닝햄 저, 비룡소)

지각대장 존은 영국의 그림 작가 존 버닝햄의 작품입니다. 맨 날 존이 늦는 이유는 다양합니다. 사자를 만나기도 하고 악어를 만나기도 하는 존은 학교 가는 길이 결코 쉽지 않습니다. 그나마 도착한 학교에서 존은 늘 사자나 악어보다 무서운 선생님을 만나게 됩니다. 선생님은 왜 존을 믿지 못하는 것일까요?

14) Mr. Late, John (John Burningham. Biryongso)

Mr. Late, John is written by John Burningham, a British painter. The reasons that John is late for school everyday are various. On his way to school, he meets a lion one day and an alligator another day. It is not easy for him to go to school without anything happened. Something even worse is that he meets a scary teacher after he gets to school safely. Why doesn't the teacher believe what John says to him/her?